A MARKED
PECULIARITY

CHARLES BACHMAN

Trafford
PUBLISHING™

Order this book online at www.trafford.com/
or email orders@trafford.com

Most Trafford titles are also available at major online book retailers.

Note for Librarians: A cataloguing record for this book is available from Library and Archives Canada at www.collectionscanada.ca/amicus/index-e.html

Printed in Victoria, BC, Canada.

ISBN: 978-1-4269-0241-3 (sc)
ISBN: 978-1-4269-0242-0 (hc)
ISBN: 978-1-4269-0243-7 (eBook)

Our mission is to efficiently provide the world's finest, most comprehensive book publishing service, enabling every author to experience success. To find out how to publish your book, your way, and have it available worldwide, visit us online at www.trafford.com

Trafford rev. 12/07/2009

Trafford
PUBLISHING®

www.trafford.com

North America & international
toll-free: 1 888 232 4444 (USA & Canada)
phone: 250 383 6864 ♦ fax: 812 355 4082

Also by Charles Bachman

If Ariel Danced on the Moon, 2006
The Strange Lives of Mr. Shakovo, 2008

For Nancy

CONTENTS

A MARKED PECULIARITY

"There is one marked peculiarity about this paper. . . ."
Charlotte Perkins Gilman, The Yellow Wallpaper

Something strange
emborders the normal
of this piece of verse
as it unwinds.

I feel a marked
peculiarity
will emerge
as words splay out,
architecture builds.

Foreordained
that a certain eccentric
design perhaps
incongruous with words

is already beginning
to show itself.

Owl
is it?
Barnyard   screech
hoot   snowy?
Iroquois bird
of ill omen?

Fluttery feathery
especially now
at night
muttering
to itself I
guess and or

what
fight-flight feelings evoking
yet

it flies downward
all hoots, claws and heaviness
into the next stanza
as it seems to spot
at the end of its descent
its prey,

strains downward
in suppressed rage
that the marks on this page

cannot contain
it.
Its anger has frightened
away its prey.

Swooping upward,
my marked peculiarity
for now
wings away.

ROUGH ROCKINESS

sometimes an edgy
   cragginess leans
      into me first thing
         in the morning first

waking, presses its
   scarpment into my soft
      semi-drowse until,
         mountain-tired, I press

down a first swirl
   of coffee, sainted rush
      beginning shortly
         and during radio music

nibbling at breakfast
   the push of cliff side
      eases becomes to my
         inner eye visible

and as the day progresses
   through tooth brushing
      dressing reading etc it
         becomes solid even
           majestic.

§

NEAR FLIGHT

Each morning
in the height of summer
the oak leaf hydrangea
   arranges the hands
at the ends of its many arms

   small cacophanies
   of patterned petals
like geese flocks of miniature
   white butterflies
   winging into
   the eastern sun.

MAPLES BEFORE RAIN

Leaden-silver underbellied leaves
shifting in wing-buffet clusters:
schools of sharply angular
paper-thin sting rays
trying to maneuver
for sustenance
in an azure
transparent
sea.

MIGRATION: THEME AND VARIATIONS

I

Compact essence of first fresh
goldenrod pollen migration
loosens in the slow breeze,
splaying out into ever more daring

designs its ever expanding
emulsion, in seconds swelling
into a gossamer magic carpet of
fine-spun gold whose delicate beauty

in seconds shatters into pattern-less
fragments of nondescript dust,
each particle answering
prayers of its mating flowers.

II

Golden crystals of pollen rise
gentle as moth wing dust
out of the flower's four-cornered pistil,
rise, a swarm of silent microbe bees
swimming on the insistent
uplift breeze of evening,

its wings steadily splaying
spreading covering farther reaches
of air as the golden swarm thins
into the ghost of a ripple,
to our seeing, apparent oblivion:

imperceptible dots of air
in silent privacy
floating down
to their waiting intended.

III

Some seeds heave out of the flower
in a sudden air perambulation
exploding into whatever wind
will carry them into whatever,

others bird-beak-bite-prone hide
their radiant profusion deep
in the winged carrier's gullet

until laved onto a new planet
where crazily their shelled essence
finds what they were meant to be.

GROOMING

After lowering myself gently down
to the merciful padded kneeler
my large garden-gloved
hands reach into
the ruffled confusion
of winterized leaves,
mostly miscellaneous maples
with kiss of chestnut, ash thrown in,

reach down into the more regular
layers beneath the surface ruffle
to grasp a larger
bundle than
the right hand
should contain,
compress it into an efficient wad,
enough to drop into the bag
between incessant gusts
of West Wind-
Ae-Pungishimook
determinedly swooping down
as when he impregnated Winona
to birth Nenabozho.

No such cosmic
drama here
as I manage to thrust
handful after handful into the bag's mouth.

Then to grasp the reassuring wood handle
of my three-prong steel bird-claw,
reaching down its gentle strength
to the liriope's
still-greenish
last-year's hair,
combing down,
out, removing leaves, detritus
leaving it clean down to the dark scalp,

dark like the all of Mother Earth's surface
I am steadily uncovering, scenting her
cool freshness
beginning to warm
from Father Sun's
intense laving
down upon her to balance impending
Thunder-beings'
evening shower
all to harmonize
within her sweet fecundity.

THE VILLAIN IS NO MORE

Jack Pokeweed has bit
the dust gone west cashed
in his chips cashed in
his checks kicked the
bucket been done in

he loomed taller and taller
in the little town where he
planted himself at first
surreptitiously then as
his stature increased so did

the mortal fear as he began
to overshadow threaten
the lovely young heroine
Red Orange Petunia
her youthful beau tall green purple

Curly Coleus not to mention
the faithful good townsfolk
inclusive of Colee-i of
other varieties but just
as curly-leaved as said beau

Curly, other Petunias of
white pink and purple hues and
hard-working purple Sweet Sue
Potato Vine and stalwart
green-leaved Vince Vinca

no sir that Jack pushed and grew till
he overshadowed all of them
then got closer so that he
started to get intertwined
into the midst of all their

doings so they could hardly
share a wind-blown-shaking-blossom-
and-leaf conversation not to
speak of not being able to
congregate without his big old

shadowing seedy self being
nearby what with him making
to the fragile banker,
all-around speculator Paul Pansy,
an offer he could not refuse

without Jack would rub his poison
self right through the guy well sir
yours truly decided it was
high time I played the deus ex
machina before this small-town

melodrama turned into some
kind of real tragic doings
so edged myself hidden-like
over the hanging pot village
and dig! cut! dry gulched

the tall varmint so to speak with
my trusty trowel so he was ready
for Pokeweed Boot Hill in a
hurry never knew what hit him
he's not buried yet but lies

wilting rotting on a hard brick
temporary bier awaiting
whatever obsequies he may
deserve. But oh the dancing and
rustlings of Miss Petunia,

young Mr. Coleus and their
colorful fellow citizens,
not to speak of the clearer view
in the town and yes a much
sweeter fragrance all around.

WHIRL

Just awake
coffee in hand I make
my way to our small pond, its
surround of cherry berry hosta,
ageratum lent enhancing vividness
by a gently generous sun
considerately

waiting for
another hour or so to
throw down its summer blister
waves, water as always in
the upper level gently whirled
by the small hose stream
breathed out from

a cairn modest,
sedate in its contrasting
stillness. As the fall of water
into the darkness adds placidity
to my placid spirit I notice bordering
this quiet oasis what must be
last night's beddings

of small creatures:
cozy, round swirls, outlines
of tiny mini-tornadoes whirling
with baby feline frenzy before settling
into nested hollows in the
newly planted grass.

FLAME

The burn of near-dusk sun
narrowed through tall grass
becomes the bright crystal
igniting all vastness
into one searing
filigree of light.

HUSKS

When in the morning,
above or without clouds
the gold orb rises,
one attempts to shuffle
off the husks that drowse
has grown in its crafty way
on the self's lean stalk,

what a jiffy-less juffle
of yankings and pullings
to try to uncover tasty truffles:
daemonic kernels of gold
lurking underneath, still,
one hopes
only muffled.

GOLDFISH

The largest-grown one
a moment ago a brief orange sheen
deep under the pond's surface,
gone in swift magician's flick
now hangs suspended
under its leaf seaweed muck refuge

all of them down there somewhere
searching frantically for safe darkness
as the incessant pump lowers their habitat,
I with long-poled net
snaring leaves, detritus
hoping to catch one unawares.

No matter how slow the net thrusts
it murks the water into safer concealment
so if one is caught
it is dumb luck,
and more good fortune
if it is held
more than momently
on the edge,
does not flip
with a relieved rush
back into darkness.

As water lowers I remove the flat rock
placed there in spring as safe harbor
from cat, heron.
I lift out the brick supports of the rock.
Their only remaining refuge
to float-crouch near
is the pump itself.

When that is lifted out
and I wait
for its smudginess
to clear,
what a riot of finning and tailing
golds the small sea on the other side
of my ensnaring tool's maneuvers.

With some patience
my net sneaks down,
its webbed mouth grabbing
two or three at one swipe
until, even after some escapes,
all eleven survivors are
tidal-waving inside the waiting bucket,
soon to return from whence
they came in spring.

If only these bright-tinted
full-grown fleeters had one tad more
wisdom in their adulthood,

were aware what was in store
at the sea life store and after:
comfort of warm tank,
then someone's aquarium,
they'd surely float languidly as water drones,
not resisting the kind threaded web,
welcoming the caring, non-fatal net.

FINE

When on a certain morning one is in fine fettle
even thickened coolness of dark-ridged cumulus
clouds seem in their interspersed streaks of brighter grey
to be seamed with almost silvery sheened metal
                    a rare bridging
                        rather than a splitting
                not glum but glittering,

when this fine fettleness lasts it streaks the very
late morning into early afternoon with small
voices sprung silvery out of the dawn mind
singing as if to reach beyond the rolling mystery
                        of weighty clouds
                    grey billowy dread
                beyond such leaden screed

beyond- post- above-cirrus into unfettered
clarity of startlingly infinite cerulean
strange emptiness that is most cogent fullness
one can never reach by anything bartered
                        by logic lame
                    as narrow-threaded, mean-
                gauged forced-fattening

of the famished spirit. Nay, let such fettle rise
fully of itself, let the rare yeast
of this uncommon day ferment as it will
because another earth-turning will follow,
                    no one can foresee
                what it in turn will be
            in its non-fine-fettled mystery.

FRAGRANCE OF MORNING

Edward arose from his bed
with a fragrant rose on his head.
It was the color of red.

His first thought, whence did it come,
this morning when he was most glum
from a night of carousing till numb.

He knew by the fragrance it was a rose.
What puzzled him was that it clung
to his forehead when up he stood, sung

his way to the mirror as was his wont.
The moment he saw it ensconced
the pain of what held it firm froze

him for moments only, then passed,
he dared not pull too hard on the curved
thorn for fear of for fear of. Beauty

is discipline, discipline beauty he said,
breaking his routine to preserve
something, heading back to bed.

SHADOW

Furry grey sphinx on the grass
stone-visaged, movement almost
imperceptible: a slight turn
of leonine head, faint focusing
of ears as he senses the barest
of curtain movement at the window
as I edge apart the lace the better
to admire his grey self.

Rising slowly to his feet,
he lumbers
toward our small patio
for morning chow.

If the mother or any of the litter five
he has fathered, scurries up
to the well-stocked dish, he will
unless ravenous, eat a modest amount
or none at all, step back almost
like a kindly grandfather

(his thirteen years or so also
qualify him for that) to let them
have their fill. Once satisfied
he lumbers slowly back to semi-statue-hood
where the sundry black and tiger five
are free to nuzzle, jump, play on,
around him until at times even

this patient Tom moves to seek
a private space. When I imitate his
slow gentleness as I approach, kneel
in slow motion, let him sniff my fingers,
oh what relaxation runs through him as
I stroke his oft-bit ears,

and as this tough, scar-aged bundle
of furred muscle--
who can break a squirrel's neck
in seconds, gorge on its carcass
till he can barely waddle--
rolls on his back in ultimate trust
presenting his belly for petting,
soft claw-retracted paws
nuzzling my hands,

his lifelong feral self yields
for these brief moments
to the breeding he was
meant for before his own
parent wandered off
or more likely was by one
of my civilized
fellow creatures
left abandoned.

SILENT SIBILANCE

In the fall when my rake
sinks its determined teeth
into strata of dry leaves,

sun, currents of air adding
wind pressure to the layering,
with what quiet shock each
year I sense, from the sudden scatter

of smallest beings in all directions
away from the center of rake-tooth
destruction, a thus-far imperceptible
country, an inter-penetration:

worm, grub, red ant, beetle tribes
all somehow strangely united for
the duration of warm weather until
my unwelcome disturbance

from their above-world at
the very time when cold is
just around the corner ready
to place its seasonal coup de grace
on their crumbling confederation.

LASSITUDINIST'S FANTASY

Autmn leaves delightful
in their soggied layerness
swirl themselves nicely
into congeries of neat piles
precisely on the curb edge

while, in concert: stone-cold hoses
come alive as kind serpents
twining their way to and through
the outer- and cellar-doors
into orderly rolls to their
nest of winter dormancy

as outdoor plant pots, assorted
statuary align themselves into
perfectly mustered columns,
marching file by file to their own
cold season barracks, to the
clipped commands of garden Diana.

MR. TRAMPOLINE SPEAKS

I am sure getting fed up by this
incessant foot-punching minute after
minute hour after hour when will they
give me a rest, let my battered skin relax

in the late afternoon breeze that is just
picking up and if they only left would
soothe one with coolness and a bit of
refreshing humidity to flex, moisten

the dry soreness. Damn here comes another
brat laughing and jumping on ouch that left
side is where they all seem to begin that
left side aching almost as much as my middle

where their crappy goal is always
to land, punching as if to deliberately
make the hurtiness even more hurty
if these blisters mushroom any more

or hatch any siblings I am going to
have to call a halt and with my last
ounce of endurance flex myself tight
then spring them all up so high their cruel feet
will spend the rest of their days
giving scaly blisters to the clouds.

THE BEAST IS BACK

Much to my later regret,
when it first became harder
to push I urged it on, noting
the only time snow blew

out of its mouth was when
I jiggled it up and down
much to the strain and drain
on arms, shoulders, and back.

My fierce beast had become
much to my chagrin
a docile domesticate
unworthy its previous name.

Stepping around its front
I noticed packed snow around
its rotary teeth, which I cleaned
with a toothpick four feet long,

then resumed again assuming
the heavy snow had been
what caused the toothed blades
to freeze their forceful chewing.

I now felt free to prod it
aggressively so to speak, rocking
it up and down as its self-propulsion
tried in vain to climb over piles

of snow, it felt to my muscles, bones,
even my brain, like trying to help
a large sluggish animal over
small mountains, one after the other.

It seemed more mobile,
its breathing sporadically
resuming, its exhales fuller
when it was able.

Yet in spite of my stronger goading,
it had apparently lost its voracious
appetite, its snow food left uneaten,
piled up, climbed over again and again.

This was confirmed when my wife
ran coatless, hatless out the door, up
to me, shouting its blades were not
turning at all, a point I argued ridiculously,

since from the kitchen window she
had been watching my entire, futile
trek down our long driveway.

Humbled at last into finally really listening,
I asked my much-more-mechanically-
minded neighbor if the rotary teeth
should ever halt while the blower

was moving forward.   No he answered
no: it needs a simple repair
of its mandibles: pins connecting
blades to axle were probably

severed. My guilt that I had caused
it to over-exert must have been palpable,
since he (epitome of human understanding)
reassured me that such was a common thing.

Nonetheless, after I had located the
new pins in the very envelope that came
with the blower, and while he inserted
them, I remained convinced

that my forcing its too vigorous
chewing against snow so deep
it should not have been challenged,
had been the heart of the problem.

Regardless, pins in place on axle,
Presto! all functions back to normal.
Almost leaping up to ride it,
I reached down affectionately to brush

off snow from its engine and housing,
as my once-more-feral bright orange beast
with the powerful cyclops headlight eye
now strode furiously down the path,

chewing, exhaling its white snow food, clearing
the driveway, restoring us (in spite of myself)
to security, freedom, mobility.

UNSEASONAL: THEME AND VARIATION

I

Without warning the wind's voice
muscles its white and crystal minions
into clusters of maple, spruce, pine
piling weight upon weight

bending arms beyond the last verge
of suppleness till they crack beneath
the hard skin down to the marrow
of the trees' bone,

the toxic breath unrelenting until
masses huddle into disabled
gaunt giants whose barked limbs
splay angular, jerk-wise
against a gradually warming sky.

II

When Boreas is early blustering in
the sharp-edged wing of his wind
it always startles, surprises, just as
we begin to savor the peaked tints

of October. This year his premature
ingress was shocking swift in its arctic
knife blade frenzy, its muscled censure
knocking, cutting through even the thick

outer barked bone of the trees' limbs
with its fury, the terrifying purity
of its wet snow, breaking down into
and through the life marrow the trees

had grown into over years, decades,
a century, now in a day and night
made cripples dangling their many arms
at odd angles in a skewed profusion
splayed out hither and yon under the white
accomplice to this devastation.

CAIRN

to build
one by one
its irregular
steps, edges
its depths
surfaces
to be
embedded
within
a slowly
evolving design
becoming whole
for a particular span
of time then one fall
morning to be seen as
tantalizingly incomplete,
a large partial seasonably abandoned

which asks
that come spring
work on its growth
be yet again resumed
toward an unforeseen
entirety discovered stone by stone
until the version which will stand when
the multi-stratified soul of my own mystery
is consigned to the hard/welcome stones of history.

LOGJAM

Sunlight shafts
bounce off
a vibrating
trampoline page
their bright projectilry
nearly blinding the eye
squinting to decipher
a poem that seems
to be about
shafts of gold
bouncing off
a poem
nearly blinding the eye
squinting
to decipher

§

TOUGH GUYS

With springing steps Robert,
five-year-old friend from the corner
and three-year almost-four me
for the very first time ever

took an adventure walk
away from our familiar block
here and there who knew where
strange streets, unknown environs,

North English, Iowa, seemed a dense,
fascinating labyrinth land
as we continued on, large house
after house until a massive building

loomed, back from the street beside
a bush-lined alley. It was immense,
junky, shed-like, and from inside
loud sloshing noises emerged

drawing us, tamping down fear, until
we found ourselves peering into
a huge mouth of wide sliding
doors at a monstrous mass moving like gills

of a giant fish—flubbering, swooshing—
gigantic red animal flesh
being cut open and into pieces with
quivering slosh-like mouths wanting to sluice

us into its shivers. Scurrying at first, Robert
and I played brave as we slowed ourselves
to a Gene Autry stride whose poise
continued until, when we opened the door

to the tea party friends of my worried mother
who said she thought we had vanished,
losing all bravado, I blurted, "We're scared
a the big monster slobbering swish swish!"

DRAIN THE CUP

So after David Tepee age nine Kenny Wilber newly-
minted eight me five, three of a total of ten kids in
100 minus population Randalia Iowa started an
excited undervoices mutter heads near each other

about the Cub Scouts what was its essence how old
one had to be to join etc I the school superintendents kid
ran home to ask my mom, proudly conveying back the news
eight was the magic age. As we continued to mull over

how one could become a full-fledged member Kenny ever
our Pathfinder Deerslayer Red Ryder Humphrey Bogart--
always wanted to "drain the full cup of life" out of any adventure--
he low-thrill-breathed into our near-clustered ears

it doesn't matter if there's a Cub Scout Troop in town,
if there isn't you become a member automatic when
you turn eight which I just did so we agreed Kenny
was already a bona fide Cub Scout which meant I guess

David was one too but him being shyer that didn't
particularly rise to the surface of our newly ripple-waved
pond of awareness. Kenny announced as a genuine
Cub Scout I'm going to start a Boy Scout Troop here

in Randalia Iowa we three constituting said organization,
which animated us no end what a way to drain the life
out of what-to-do boredom day after hot summer day
in and around the small burg never enough kids for even

a real baseball game. But Kenny averred to his thrilled
wondering followers to get in official-like there's an initiation.
Its gonna be hard but will prove what we're made of. First off
he led us near the train tracks to the twenty yards of creosote-

soaked railroad ties butted end to end blazing hot in the sun.
I could see David's enthusiasm cooling a bit like mine as we
looked down at our shoed feet and then at Kenny's,
toughened from going bare-footed all summer and

this was mid July. But the whole thing psyched us up too much
to pull out now and besides we couldn't back down what would
the likes of Sky King the Green Hornet the Lone Ranger think
so okay well Kenny said first part is you have to walk barefoot

the whole length of the rail ties then jump feet first into that low
pile of gravel at the end. The sun suddenly seemed a whole lot
hotter everywhere as David and I took off our shoes and watched
our pathfinder walk not run over the blistering ties then jump high

landing feet first in the pile of sharp-edged small rocks.
David first then me as fast as fiery pain could push us over the
Herculean trek then ow ow ow into shards of stone more pain
some blood Kenny waiting there to congratulate us what next

we asked he thought a minute lets take it slow play cops and robbers
today, undergo the second part tomorrow. Next morning barely
dashing down breakfast I dashed off sore feet notwithstanding to Kenny's
for the news: smoking cigarettes under the bridge. Wrinkle-browed

thinking by my two older friends then a solution: Me as
five-year-old son of the superintendent of schools walk
to Wilson's General Store ask Mrs. Wilson innocent-like
for a pack of Lucky's for my dad and throw in the free small

box of matches if you don't mind which clutching the coins
Kenny and David provided, I did no problem, seeing Mrs.
Beeman on the way back to the bridge her asking, "Chuck
what you got in the paper bag, candy?" Me replying "This isn't

candy this is cigarettes!" moving into a run toward the bridge.
David and Kenny lit up and puffed not telling me how, I thought
my finding out must be part of the inititiation so I pulled one out of
the pack stuck it in my mouth the way they did, bit into it trying

to chew some of the tobacco awful spit it out threw the cig into
the creek
they taking pity I guess declaring that was good enough I had passed
this part of the test as they continued for awhile we're draining
the life
out of these cigs just like we're draining the full cup of life down to

the dregs out of our new adventure smiled Kenny, I didn't know
what dregs meant but it sounded Humphrey Bogart-like
which was enough for me. One more ordeal he said, the big word
sounding secret and powerful to our fraternal ears so next day

Immersion into Full Scouthood, on to the pond on David's farm
undressed threw our clothes on the muddy fence waded in,
them to their waists me half way up to my neck in water so dark
from hog lot runoff you couldn't see your hand a few inches underneath.

Dance around Kenny ordered in a churchlike chant we did our best in
the thick water feeling the muck squeezing like threatening
quicksand into our toes Arise from Your Child Prison he ordered
so we climbed
out onto the cow-tracked shore of this lake of transformation

each of us encrusted with fifteen to twenty bloodsuckers on most
body parts we needed no command to commence pulling them
off each other's twitching skin so the life would be drained out of them
before they drained it out of us ha ha rhetorized Kenny, clothes back on.

We ran to Kenny's house where he announced we are now the official
first ever Randalia Iowa USA Planet Earth Boy Scout Troop
as our Kool-Aid cups of life ranneth over
and we drained them down to the final dregs.

PLEASANTVILLE CRUSADES

Jolly were we Bobby Patch other friends and I
so light of foot
we floated on
currents of electric expectation
home from another unmemorable day

in Pleasantville, Iowa, second grade (I think I studied
subtraction) into
what really mattered:
resonating through the radio's wooden house,
wondrous waves of ear-tingling

mingles of fear anxiety relief dread as we
entered the rugged
Canadian wilderness
part of every horse's trot
and gallop with deep-voiced Sergeant Preston

of the Royal Mounted Police as our always dignified hero
chased down
his villain in
whatever far-flung neck of rock
or foliage he might be hiding. Then presto we flew

with air ace Sky King in blue, stormy skies
only our wonder
could conjure as he
with immense velocity of his trusty
Piper Cub and hawkeye vision spotted them,

quickly pointed the nose of his craft into a near-
death-defying
dive amid
bullets from desperate desperadoes
near whom he landed, bounded out with his faithful

friend, ensnared the scoundrels in the sure web
of radio justice.
And then after
as quick a supper as would satisfy
the insistent table protocol of my

genteel mother, me streaking out the house to enact what
and who I had heard,
along with their thrilling
comic book counterparts: such wonders
as Wonder Woman strong, achingly lovely,

lithe but powerful Green Hornet, Captain Marvel
and their like
who also solved
mysteries, ferreted out, swooped
down on, across at hawk-faced moral uglies.

Now us friends out in my own back yard up
the ladder into
the loft of our fireman's/
policemen's/ detectives'/ wonder-rescuers'
den of virtue--it masquerading as an old

chicken house—whisper conferring as to who
would be good guys
who the bad,
the good remaining aloft until
the bad had shimmied down the steel pole

and vamoosed to wait in parts unknown, then
down shimmied
the good to fly at,
gallop toward, ferret out
their nasty selves, sometimes as the Lone

Ranger with Tonto (once a week savored treasure)
guns blazing
at contentious cohorts
of evil who blazed back until
they were plugged, routed, arrested, incarcerated

in our secure jail alias former hog shed,
there to remain
as the world racked
by the likes of Tojo, Hitler, Mussolini
was rendered clean once again.

BRO

Another summer day in Gray,
sandwiches, watered canteens packed
in dad's World War II knapsack,
fishing poles, hopeful stringer that may

or may not hold riches come
the effortful day's end, but try
we had to as we loaded our small selves in spry
fashion onto our dusty Schwinns.

But this was one of those mornings when Pat
Aikman and I had an added responsibility
for our Thunder Creek enterprise: my three-
year-old brother Lyle, with mother solicitude

decked out even in this heat in
coveralls o well as his guarantor
I was glad to boost him up to the bike bar
that would safely carry us off, down

the cracked asphalt hill street past
modest houses, our Methodist Church,
farther down the slope the Church
of God where rumor had it weird goings-

on transpired behind frosted
windows (frosted, we had heard
from most venerable town elders,
precisely to conceal the strange rites

of holy-rollerdum: shouting
unearthly noises, beating of breasts,
God knows what arcane moves
of bodies in that enclosure). We winged

our way so to speak down from
there to the hill's foot: post office,
city locker, defunct bank where clots
of old man Davis' suicide blood

had shone under an oak the morning
we moved to town, meaning
our four-member family had comprised
a net gain of three to the hundred-minus

souls of Gray, Iowa. Back across
the dirt road, exciting because Schwarz'
Café had recently opened across the lot
from the omnipresent bar I was not

allowed to enter. On the other side
again, multi-tasking general store,
then Shoemakers' gas station: the greater
extent of railroad-closed Gray's inner

city. Soon, bikes carefully
leaned against the bridge's upper
railing, we squat-lowered our way
down the craggy bank to our big river,

a nomenclature we appended
because the creek once small, fishless,
had in the last year through floods
from heavy rains had a miraculous growth spurt

into a broader, deeper, faster moving
something of mystery now locked in the lore
of the town's memory. Our ten-year-old minds
soared each time we approached this fish-full wonder,

as now we sat: worm-baited hooks
descending into moving darkness,
Pat, myself, Lyle between
(his three-year-old awe no doubt the most extreme

of our small company). Pat moved
a few steps away to try his luck.
As my bobber floated a bit downstream,
for a few moments my glance followed.

Casually turning: beside me empty space.
Staring with heart-race into the murky water:
my brother's blonde hair
waving with the current
a foot beneath the surface,
not yet swept downstream.

In one panicked motion throwing
down my pole, I lean-reached
my right hand into his curls, pulled
until I could grasp under his arms,
totter-tug him up and out,

soused as a wet cat, sputtering
wide-eyed, scared but safe. Sitting him
well up the bank, I gave him
a wet hug, asked was he all right,

yes piped his three-year-old voice
yes okay. Okay I heard myself say
as if in a dream. Okay. Okay.
I had Pat ride him away

home as I re-checked my hook,
the wiggle of wormed bait,
re-cast my line, looking ahead
to some quick bites
of perch or at least bullhead.

PAT AIKMAN

I

If only I could lay a glove on him
I yearning each time at recess,
he at nine my ten-year-old
pugilist self's opponent within
the ring layered with eager peers
egging us on in our allowed
three-round encounter.

My dad, "professor" superintendent,
coach, history teacher of the tiny
consolidated school at Gray, Iowa,
encouraging our boyhood bent
toward boxing, of which mine
may have been one of the most intense,
but all of us

heating into it with more sheer
pleasure than can be surmised
by one who has not known
the adrenaline rising as the eyes
of one's opponent shift to the side
only a little, a clue that a feint
there, then a quick jab
on the other side may nail him.

Pat always my eternal frustrator.
Smaller, weaker, with fairly prominent chin,
a seeming easy mark,
yet time and time again
whatever my strategy,

at the last split second
his dodge would save him
from my gloved fists,
my powerful right
that most yearned
to have at his face
but never did.

II

His stock: pretty smart,
mom Wilma former teacher,
dad Glen intellectual hog dealer,
both, ethics personified,
yet Pat in school sometimes
suddenly pisser-mooded
as if from a yen for riling,

leading, a couple of afternoons,
(I non-participating approver)
to corrective after-school peer
de-pantsing, him running home
in skivvies, said pants held as ransom.

III

What did he and I not play,
good and lively friend
in a tiny dusty town
where playmates were few
and far between?

Buying a garter snake, catching
two more, showing our folks,
dad with his phobia
saying "Out of here with that thing!"
Transporting Willie our favorite
with his two compadres
Mike and Eddie
back to Pat's yard, sitting
the bucket down, finding
after a ten minute nature call
the trio had vamoosed to parts unknown.

Our first Red Ryder BB guns
we new-made-men trying out
together on menacing bushes,
sparrows and such, and we
metamorphosing into cowboys
down by Thunder Creek,
its steep dirt embankments

seeming to us the veritable
mountain crags upon and around
which Gene Autry Roy Rogers
Tim Holt Johny MacBrown
Hopalong Cassidy Charles Starrett as
the Durango Kid

would hot pursue, shoot or arrest
respective varmints
in thriller westerns
shown every Friday night
on the tavern wall
in good weather.

Horse-galloping our dusty shoes,
pulling cap revolvers with swift
menace out of genuine leather
holsters as need arose,
like the time Pat "rode" ahead of me
up and along our high-bank mesa,
disappeared in a cloud of summer dust,
me rushing up to the edge

peering down to see him lying
beside the squarish rock
he had fallen on. To our relief
he was okay, we building it into
our battle with Hopalong's enemies:

His palomino having been shot
out from under him, Pat almost
"bit the dust" as he bit the rock's dust,
which would have made
villains mighty glad.

He, okay after that rock mishap,
the look on his face before the game
resumed, was not of play. About
that look I wondered awhile then forgot

until, a year after I left the town
his sister Linda spun their car
off the road down a much steeper
embankment, throwing Pat out
midway through the plunge
from which he was not okay,
from which there was no
return to the game.

SMOKING CORN STEMS WITH GERALD YOUNG

The hardest thing was making it
across the Young's barnyard—that space
between the capacious barn, chicken shed
and milkhouse—at 2 PM or thereabouts,

that being during the period
of time it was contested territory
if any small boys entered it:
the banty rooster had his eyes peeled

for any threats to his harem of plump,
clucking peckers and scratchers: if he caught
out of his wrinkled eye-sockets, a glimpse
of us, all twenty-six ounces of red-

cockled, crimson-feathered beaked
fury would launch itself boy-ward, claws
at the ready for sliced punishment.
So as always we bided our time, whispers

at the gate being the only sound until
his florid majesty had made his slow,
unharried way to the far corner locale
near the hall of his roosting-nest chateau.

We moved from a slow creep into a run,
hearing his rooster-testosteroned chatter
as we hurried through the double doors of the barn
up the ladder into the atmosphere

of the scratchy-soft sun-shaft pierced hayloft.
I had my contribution of boxed matches,
Gerald supplying the corn stems—the soft,
moist narrow stalk offshoots with kiss

of open field still in their odor.
Would its taste fulfill that promise?
Lounging back like men of a larger sphere,
we lit up our Cuban stogies till the ends

seemed to gleam with the glory of red
ash, then as one man we took our first
puff, mine of course not the least bit
tentative, erupting into a burst

of coughing I tried to quiet down
'cause if we were caught—we won't go there.
Gerald, obviously older and wiser at eleven
years to my ten, took it slower

much to my admiration. That afternoon
we lit and re-lit many times,
whispering the marvel of dizzying swoon
that cig by cig clouded our space

till we had gone through at least six
apiece, barely a thought in our minds' eye
that one of the matches or stems
might fall into the dry bed of hay,

but mostly concerned, since it was getting
on to dusk, whether we could in stupor
make our way down the ladder, to our homes
without stumbling, or losing our afternoon
in an unheroic up-chuck at supper.

FOUND OUT

Trying somehow to be inconspicuous
as a small toad on a mottled grey rock,
I huddled behind the six boys ages
nine through twelve, wishing for more dark

from a sky that was far too moon-lit,
having, the group of us, fooled around
with a school basement window, heard it
snap open, started to run, paused to listen.

Hearing nothing the oldest boy had ventured
inside, we standing guard as it were
especially since my house, my father's, stood
across the dirt road, sending a slight shiver

into our improvised adventure, my dad
being school superintendent and all.
Just after coming back out, the lad
who had entered, in whispered thrall

was regaling us with ghost possibilities
when my father's baritone wafted resonant,
tearing into our suddenly-sobered spines,
"You boys get over here this instant!"

There he stood, the bright porch light
outlining him in silhouette.
It being 1947, an Iowa small town,
no one scattered and ran, let alone
acted rebellious, none emitted a breath
of disrespect, such would have been death

to our pride. So there I slouched, from time to time
peering out as he skillfully gleaned
from our leaders what had been done,
allowing in his firm but reasoned

manner the fact that the window had
flown open, we had not broken in,
true, oh true we should not have been
there at all, let alone pushing at it,

we were at fault no doubt and very sorry
yes he responded, nodding his head
as his eyes just then looked through me
but his rhythm and tone didn't miss a beat.

I had expected a surge of fear because
of who I was, but as he continued his slow
dialogue with us, I felt strangely safe
somehow within his speech's tone and flow

as he meted out our punishment: curfew
at seven pm for a month except for youth
church meetings. What for young people now
would have elicited an angry oath

at such unfairness, evoked a relieved sigh
in each one of us, knowing why
we more than deserved it, me being
even more aware how he as pre-adolescent
had played some pranks that made this one
seem mild indeed.   So there was precedent.

But looking back now, that did not account
for the strange feeling of safe harbor I had
even as he looked at my delinquent
self in the darkness behind the other lads.

Now, looking out into my own night
long after his passing, that porch light
behind his face sends a sudden shaft
of recognition through me, the lift

of a long-drawn curtain which shows me now
beyond doubt's shadow the mix of two scenes
in my then and long-after mind, and their collision
threatens to skew the drama, disallow

the way together they might encompass
something I now know, which peels
away encrusted layers of conscience,
giving me more than pause:
Not once over the years did I ever say
how safe that and all nights he made me feel,
and that it came out of the man he was.

AUNT MARIE

As elder of two daughters (by ten years)
among seven sons, and ultra-responsible,
she understood that the expected way
was marry a good man, it not being probable

apparently that her career would move
beyond teaching in a country school,
which after high school she had managed
for two years, the unspoken rule

for her time and gender not likely
to encourage college, let alone
the future that three brothers would pursue:
osteopaths treating muscle, bone,

advancing just as had their legend aunt
(their mother Jennie, second generation
Dutch, did always speak of her younger sister
Dr. Emma with a twinkle of admiration).

Marie, one of the brightest of the lot,
ever-curious, avid reader of books,
lively of mind and person, full of challenge:
I can well remember the startled looks

on the faces of adolescent boys who came
to "Trick or Treat" on Halloween, only
to be confronted by Aunt Marie insisting
it was "Trick FOR treat." Suddenly lonely,

on an unwelcome stage, with an audience
more scary than any goblins or ghouls
on the growly prowl this All-Hallows Eve,
they saved themselves from being complete fools

by doing something, often prompted by
Marie: a funny face, a snatch of song,
or when every other inner resource
failed, a definitely not over-long

nursery rhyme called up in desperation.
To behold a youth whose voice in midst of change
recited the whole of "Ba ba black sheep," was
for me as a young boy as edgily strange

as any trick or treating I had done.
Sitting there was the kind, good-natured man
she had decided to marry at nineteen,
Harold the farmer, whose talk seldom outran

his daily concerns with hogs, cows, sheep,
as Marie, glancing down at the calloused knuckle
he got fencing in young lambs that fall,
exchanged with this love of her life a heart-felt chuckle.

STEVE BERRY AND I: GHOSTERS

It was a dark but not stormy night,
Steve Berry and I slowly making
our way from my house across town
to his, him beginning:
"It was a dark and stormy night."

As the tale developed our tails
moving faster under festering
shreds of cloud here and there
sludging in front of a near-half moon,
"When suddenly there appeared— "

We two, teller and listener, frissoning
to a sudden halt, listening.
Peering around, especially behind.
What was that rustle?
"—from what seemed a mere rustle

of leaves behind them, a strange— "
Accelerating steps, Steve's
house in sight, until there, his porch,
his older sister Glenna, reassuring
mentor in all things mystical,

his young brother Tommy, who had once
interrupted our seance, his mom and
sister Connie talking inside, his dad
sitting comfortably in their book-lined
living room. Tommy and Glenna going inside,
we too tough to beg her to stay. Alone for seconds

of stillness, Steve breaking it to finish:
"The two of them ran screaming
from the heinous thing that reached
out, touching its cold fingers to
their necks as it almost caught

them, then did, and dragged them
away. They were never seen again."
Pause, cookies and pop.
Me uttering, Steve, could you walk me
home? That was a walloper.
Sure, best friend.
Heading out into the darkness,
me taking my inevitable turn: "There
had always been something strange
about the old Murphy mansion standing
like a grim sentinal on that corner— "

The old Murphy mansion hoving
into sight. "But especially on this
cloud-scudded night it seemed somehow— "
Our steps seeming to grind
against the sidewalk's bone-chalk grit.

"From that densely-wooded corner came
two simultaneous sounds: one eerily raspy,
thoaty, the other as of a heavy object being
dragged along gritty sand." We as if tacking
for hours across wind, arriving at my porch.
Parents, young brother Lyle reading inside.

"The wraith-like figure moved
in the corner upstairs window every
Halloween after John's untimely death."
Silence, a rest, staring at the night
and each other. Chuck, I wouldn't mind
some company walking home. Sure.

His turn again:
"Surely that large narrow object
that had just flown by his face was
nothing but--" A whirl of what we hoped
were sand flies noising itself at our backs,
we trudging on, on.

"But the small boy had never
seen a dragonfly, or any insect
for that matter, that whizzed by
with quite such bulk."
We spectre-ridden friends now rushing.

"The boys' bodies were never found,
only the shell of the largest, strangest
flying insect the town had ever seen." Steve,
I could sleep here at your house on the floor.
No, we've got an extra bed. Spend the night.

DUST ENGRAVER

As next-to-youngest laid off from pouring concrete
"the youngest" two will go said the boss, me
at seventeen definitely did fit

that bill, but nodded politely, knowing Lee
the sixteen-year-old was the boss's grandson, so
would be taken back on in some capacity

what the hell tough life lesson, so
moved on, by chance finding myself headed
west with a touch of old romantic hobo

in me with Fred and his cousin Glenn, Fred's
family having worked for One-eyed Charlie
who owned a big Colorado peach orchard

wait'll you see the number sevens gleefully
averred Fred they're bigger than any peach
you've ever seen in Iowa, these are peewees

that's for sure. We headed off, the itch
for adventure and for dollars we were desperate
for, pushing us to an energetic pitch

of hopefulness. After a two-day jaunt
in Fred's Chevvy we checked in with One-Eyed Charlie
who didn't bother getting up, intent

as he was on the TV screen, an inductee
into the lodge of wrestle-mania,
cheering for Injun Joe, now designee

of the mantle of heroism, whose new reign
could end tonight by Killer Kowalski, whose spree
of mayhem had led him to take off the ear of one

of his recent opponents. On the mantel is your first-floor key
yelled Charlie. After settling in nothing
for dinner except what we brought: Campbell's pea

soup we heated and downed. Later driving
through the orchards seeing meandering lights
Fred, who'd been here before said they're getting

their supper--Oakies and Mexicans every night.
A few days later with most peaches entering
their ripening stage we were assigned our alloted

tasks Fred picking Glenn and I dumping
into the hopper. On one of our breaks I sauntered
around a little, till near one overhang

slouched a skinny sallow-faced man bib-overalled
as his bony son sat in a dry patch
of dust. To a straight-backed, clean-dressed, better-fed

gent, the Oakie pled this kid of mine is a match
for any, fourteen, a strong worker you can trust
him for anything—as the small twig arms stretched
to draw circle after meandering circle in the dust.

AT NIGHT ON MOUNT GARFIELD

And what good was a pin-prick flashlight
in this unknown arena of sun-parched rocks,
gravel, scrub bush, crags ridged with sharp teeth
poised around the mouth of some ravine

lurking in blind darkness for one to
stumble into? Dammit new-made-lawyer
Glenn McGee, where the hell did you
disappear to? Cocky we had been to announce

at supper to our fellow soon-to-be
peach-pickers that we would venture
to climb that looming,
"non-challenging" mountain

that very evening, packing our knapsacks
with flashlights, bread, eggs, bacon,
even salt and pepper to flavor
the do-or-dare cuisine of our plan.

Hadn't even forgotten, each of
us, World War II Army
blankets to complement the Army
mess kits, silverware and full canteens.

Well-prepared! And to boot having
promised to ignite a bonfire beacon
on the lofty night-dark ledge of the
summit we had no doubt we'd attain,

so in a few hours, friends, glance out
the window facing Garfield every ten
minutes or so to notate the bright
sign that we have fulfilled our big dare,

have conquered, are surveying the vastness
of our visual kingdom, will be ensconced
under the stars in slumber until
sun-up's height-enhanced taste of bacon,

etc. and we lazily make our way
back in triumph, tranquility
of mind and spirit, back to mundane
matters of preparation for mere

picking, loading, etc. of peaches
to pay for our adventures. But why
did Glenn and I, panting from the climb
up countless ridges of rock and sand,

having rested every hundred steps
to let lungs catch up, why did we,
aside from impatient frustration
at not having detected a clear

summit, why did we choose
to "briefly" separate,
he moving around

a crag to ascertain
whether the view
would be more
promising
from that
place,

both of us sure we couldn't help
but be able to recognize
that particular crag in the un-
likely event that we lost our or-

ientation. Ha ha we had joked
ha ha maybe a tad over con-
fident but we were sure we'd never
be out of earshot of each other

I shouted Glenn Glenn
Glenn: some panic
crescendoing,
the stark enclosure
of the dark mountain's
small mesa shrinking by the minute.

Maybe I'll have to spend
this night on my lonesome
with no bare slab on which
to build a fire, for—are
there beasts in this kind
of scrub-crag wilderness?

In a burst of sanity
I made up my mind to confine
my movement to this graspable space
so at least one of us was anchored
as it were, a steady place-stayer

around which the other could move
in orbit, hoping he had homing
instincts primevally superior
to my woeful sense of direction

which I hadn't bothered to warn him
about before we initiated our dark trek.
One more shout--a hulking menace
appearing around the the crag just left

of the largest scrub. I shined my light
into the face of Glenn who shined
back, gravel-crunched toward me,
looking peaceful, confident,

as he matter-of-factly declared,
from where he had been, one could behold
what appeared to be the definite
summit. Forcing a coolness into

my larynx, I nodded manly-like:
Excellent, Glenn, I'll follow you out
there to the left where I figured you'd
find the view we needed.

CUTTINGS

I

Sunspots must be
on the move again
or am I these last few
cycles of luna
a magnet for woe?

Things too manifold
to be merely
rare,

situations become
suddenly their own
paradigms as my
fellow-creatures and I
move porpoise-like
through dim waters,

chance becomes
more than chance,
a net of unknown
dimensions to catch
the plainest, most colorful
beings of disaster.

Finely-meshed
in selected places
wavering in
at odd moments
it seems to enfold anything
but the expected.

Severed tendons,
surgeon-quick umbilical
cuttings leaving drift,
distance.

II

When my mother passed over
after a steady, raw-edged,
temporarily winning
quarrel with her ending,
when the parasitic flower
suddenly began again
to bloom, generate
life against life
as she fought
to bring a healing
winter to her blood,
to freeze the expanding
spring within her,

the season as all
such seasons
was merciless as it blossomed
(Not even Hades could have halted it then)
carrying all before it
like a green-robed queen.

III

Thinking of
nets,
sea life,
I look
outside
for other
spring, wondering
why a friend
from down under
was in New Orleans
splattered by a stranger's
sock full of lead.

Why a family web of destiny
was so constructed
another friend
almost ended it
in America's heartland,
her family so wholesome
they could not come to her
even *in extremis,*

But rather flew
to the southern sun
for their annual pleasured
interlude.

Why an acquaintance and another friend
have the first bright sproutings
of the same exotic spring flower
that bloomed my mother's life away.
Why parasitic lovelies flowered out
the skulls of two mothers of friends.

IV

Orestes, Cassandra, are you in some way
companions of the small modern human
who spreads these netted lines
over the page?

Or might it be possible
by clever maneuvers
to delay the grasp of the
close-webbed, corded hands
or by swimming hard, mercilessly,
to pierce on through
into the clear water beyond?

ACCIDENT

Green light ahead
street name familiar
place unfamiliar
make my way
in a very short while
home.

Left turn
to cross the highway
left neck turn
too late,

Maroon cyclone
crimson tornado
roar of reddish pickup
careening toward me
honking, brakes screeching
me quickly wrenching
the steering wheel right
to lessen
the sure impact
fear

split-second bracing of self
sharp crush
metal to metal
into my shoulder
pushing my car like an unmoored skiff.

This has not happened:
nightmare
close the eyes, open them,
close again

just need to
rewind the tape, pause,
play it again
re-open eyes
the tape
will not rewind.

Right foot feeling
outside the door
for solid ground
alive or is this
another dream
walking when
I should be
extinct or paralyzed:

within seconds
two layers of reality
seeing, eye-connecting
with the other driver,
"Darn," he says, "darn!"

Me: I don't see how this happened.
Him: There were No-Left-Turn signs there,
he calling police
me now knowing there's no debate,
saying once I'm sorry.

Now unfolds the full scene
I've noted many times
as a driving-by non-involver:
police sedans, ambulance,
vehicles metal-mutilated,

uniformed querying
what happened
any witnesses etc.
me always sorry
for those unfortunate ones
caught in such swirl
hoping there were no injuries or worse,

now I am the one
whose unsure body
is supported
into the open side mouth
of the ambulance.

Shoulder muttering with pain
sitting, blood-pressure taken
questions they always asked another:
Dizzy? hands fingers arms legs toes moveable?
them feeling my back and abdomen:

Internal pain?
them calling report in
asking which hospital

I replying
while once more
shutting out the light
once more
some one else
must be playing
this role in
a TV ER scene.

Real ER: opposite me
my anxious wife
tamping down qualms
to give reassurance.

No more media nightmare
shoulder pain shouldered aside
by a stinging self-blame
that seems
it will forever
unpoise, unpoise,
eating, eating away

as, in the car
I hang on the raw edge
of vigilance
for drivers
as bad
as myself.

POETRY RECITATION: SUITE IN TWO MOVEMENTS

I. Andante Cantabile

It is all scheduled for an official-kind of place.
A semi-intimate setting where other readings have been.
A kind of college student union building with many rooms.
Armed with eating and recreating places bookstore etc.

This event is advertised as me reciting from memory
a poem by little-known poet E.K. Beaton.
I am anticipating my reading.
I think its special appeal is the poem will come from memory.
Not the printed page.
There is something fascinating about that.
As when you tell rather than read a story.

The Student Union area is unusually aswirl abuzz.
I am delayed by dining lines etc., other busy-ness of some sort.
It is fifteen minutes past my opening time.

A grey-haired distinguished connoisseur walks by me.
He is leaving thinking it has been cancelled.
I tell him no I am on my way.
I follow him back toward the designated room.
The hallway is long.

When we get there I am twenty minutes late.
A few people patiently wait.
A few are about to leave.
When they see me arrive I have a thick anthology.

Inside just for reference lurks said poem.
Most of them with little fanfare go back to their seats.
I try to stride with purpose up to the podium.
I open the book to that poem just in case.

I chat informally with my audience.
Some of them are now milling about.
Beaton's name does not appear in the book's index.
His name has been scissored out of the table of contents.

II. Allegro Agitato

The grey-haired man seems to be leaving I follow oh oh
back from the long hallway I am twenty minutes late
a few wait some almost leave they see me arrive with
my thick anthology with the poem in it for safety
to the podium I try to stride opening the book just for
safety bullshitting with the people some mill about

IsearchbutBeatonsnameisnowheredont panic keep
searchinghisnameisscissoredoutIaskmyseatedwifewhere
shesaysshedoesntknowohoh I forget poem must con-
tinue improvising cool I hope chattingchattingchatting
re parodistic import etc my brain on two tracks at once—

for myself why the hell did you all come here to hear
only one poem—to them "serious" performances may be
intended as self-parody even travesty or
burlesqueburlesqueburlesque is in the eyes of colleagues
fellow poets Davids Lampe, Landrey now I'm in for it
omigodtheyregivingmethumbsupforagreatsatirical show.

VICTORIA SINGING

When asked
up she stands
a teen
suddenly adult-poised,

as her mother begins on piano
her smile's radiance
almost fills the room

even before the first
clear notes
well-phrased words
float out of her

filling the entire space
with a shimmer of bright
vibrating jewels.

KEYS TO LIVING

and after they in white waiter/waitress garb
had passed the trays of veggies broccoli beans
carrots peppers green and red then they with
continuing smiles distributed sheets of paper
with big round O's on them must be we said

substitutes for squash maybe for a later exchange
recalling my earlier "exchange" after a few hours
of holding onto the entire set of keys belonging
to Art Dean head of all audiovisual equipment
at the college, me puzzled at myself that needing

one of the keys I hadn't simply asked, but just
seen them lying on his desk and temporarily
borrowed them so to speak and then after a few
hours my god what was he to do and how was I
to get them back without being accused of—

anyway I had brazened my way into his office
hoping he wasn't there but he was there, so quick
improviso I halely heartily averred that my set of
keys looked so much like his I must have picked up
his inadvertently, other people there present also,

Art acting like no problemo dude and look Art said,
at this stone breaker, showing me an implement with
five or six mean-looking screwdrivers of various sizes

and lengths sticking out of it yeah I said what a stone-
breaker then left glad to be out of there and then

the trays of veggies with O-drawn paper as *piece
de resistance* so to speak O how did I end up with
this after the all of the all of that?

FLYING INTO BOSTON

I

Now and then
the winding grey path
far beneath the plane's silver wing
appears in the shine
of intermittent morning light,
disappears when each
shaft of light is severed:

magic, transformative serpent,
ancient inscription
continually lost
each time it is about
to be deciphered.

II

Pockets of serpentine-bordered
moltenness,
azure-mirrored,
reflect back waves
of diffused cloud light
while keeping possessive grip
on captive brown foam islands.

III

The flat, dark blue Leviathan
holds its sharp-nosed body
steady in its snug surround
of green-treed ocean,
its only visible movement:
ripples along its wave-scale skin.

DOWN THE IPSWICH RIVER

Slow-moving, leisurely with the slow-moving
current me more leisurely than my two sons,
Eric in the stern, the elder Nicolai in the bow
of the long canoe, soft splash of their paddles
me in the middle not paddling, free to chat, observe,

I feeling almost as still as the Heron poised like
a well-postured, grey-suited French maître d'
welcoming us with steady, un-sycophantic eye
into his weedy, thin-treed hotel enclave around
the first bend in our wide water journey,

we three travelers, not quite weary enough yet
to assent to his welcome, nonetheless observing
his unhurried dignity as Eric pointed out in
hushed tones he was indeed a Grey Heron,
deserving of all the respect his manner signified.

Conversing in words sprung from our relaxed
natures on such an adventure, first for all
three of us, even as we had to be careful here
and there for friction-prone rocks,
fallen trees, logs, etc., this continuing

after we temporarily beached so I could spell
Nicolai in the bow. While on land: two young
men in the other canoe apparently heading
down the wrong stream, telling us they took
the proper left turn at the fork, but encountered

a mass of brush that looked like they couldn't
get through. We: We'll try the proper left
turn as the canoe owners instructed. Those two:
heading their own way anyway, we seeing from
a wise look down that long, straight channel, that

if they had taken the wrong turn, they wouldn't discover
it for at least two-thirds of a mile. Me in the bow,
approaching the infamous wall of brush, spotting
on the left a possible slip-through spot, we with heads
bent low, some grinding and rubbing, gingerly gliding

without a scratch between our mini-Scylla and Charybdis,
a small triumph which we three Odysseus types duly
cheered ourselves for. On flowed the words through ambient
water, sky, still and moving beings, I noting with wry
professorese, this might be James Dickey's Deliverance

country, better watch out, even here in Massachusetts,
laughs all around, Dr. Eric, researcher, former youth
herpatologist, continuing as our warm guide to natural
plant, winged, and swimming wonders, including
an even hoarier, more reserved guest-greeter
which he explained was in its Snowy Egret nature.

On we flowed with the slow river past two magnificent
snapping turtles that loomed like threatening
rocks, having no interest in observing let alone greeting
or inviting us, unlike the model-thin Cormorant peering
just before spreading its ample wings and heading

into a sycamore, Nicolai--noble-spirited
with inner riches of Sanskrit, Yoga, and Ayurveda—
observing that in not flying too far its spirit might
have sensed our generous presences, we
patting ourselves on the back, concurring.

All of it—
beaching half-way down, so my boys in their
forties, could fly chortling in tire swings out,
over, into the welcoming current, both in their turns
etched in the just-before-letting-go dusk, hardly
distinguished from the local teens in the prime
of youth-fresh adventuredom

which all three of us were--
as our on-flow melded us into this generous nature,
melded us forever into each others' natures.

STONE WALL OF HOUSE

Eric and Lisa's house, Swampscott, Massachusetts

I

Cluster of rocky islands
in a concrete grey sea.

II

Jagged, dirt-encrusted ice floes
jamming into menace
on an accelerating river.

III

Massive coarse-grained craggy hailstones
avalanching down
a sheer grey
sky mountain.

FLIGHT DELAY

4:25 a.m.: clock radio and cell phone alarm
conspire, plunging me into
a dark middle-of-the-night abyss,
I work quickly to shovel my way
up through its strata of thick marl
into some semblance of coffee-less consciousness

more or less succeeding
in the zombie robotics
of minimal breakfast,
austere ablutions.

5:20 a.m.: my son Nicolai and I
cab-whisked away to Logan Airport
me for my 7:30 to Buffalo
him for his 7:50 to Albuquerque then Santa Fe,
dropoff, goodbyes.

6:20: boarding pass already printed,
quickly through security,
relax into a seat at my gate,
transforming from ouch how early
to smiled anticipated reward:
Buffalo by 9:00.

Vicious voice
dread red sign:
delay till 10.

In line at the counter.
Answer: plane arrived late last night
safety rest requirement, good but—
shall I bother to query
how it got to be late last night
how the cause-effect chain was linked
how we got to be on this earth
how the universe began
to hell with this
mud-brained squirmy snarl.

The moment has come to kill
this long turd worm of time
by chopping it into small segments.

Too sleepy yet to continue Les Murray's poems
so catch a right-angle-neck-bent snooze,

wake at 7,
Snips: snatches of reading, peregrinations
between coffee and muffin (used up a half hour)
men's john (thank gods I had to go:
another fifteen minute segment snipped,
flushed down the vast toilet
that transforms present to past)
notify Nancy of the delay.

Sit, snooze, read, sip:
I snip each swathe.
Watching them fall one by one
the worm mass slowly shortens.
Sit, snooze, read, sip
start this rambling mock epic.

Boarding
I'll finish this
all right
last snip:
the mud-colored
remnant coils
in the final flush
out of sight.

WRAITHS ON INDEPENDENCE DAY

Fireworks on the Fourth:

Expanding vari-colored
light-flecked spheres.

Multi-fingered luminescent hands
arching downward:
glowing segmented yellow-white
branches of willow trees
bending into the Niagara River.

Splayed-out octopus arms
swarms of glimmer-red fireflies
exploding nebulae.

Behind the cosmological convulsion
mammoth grey ghost spiders
darkening as they drift southward
toward the slivered horned moon
transforming into
blackish clouds
of vague interstellar mist.

POSTURE

Pale roses droop
under spring drizzle:
Ballerinas at prayer.

§

MOUNTAIN FACE

Where yesterday a grand carapace of stone
looked calmly across the crevasse, now a ridge
grimaces in choppiness, a bone
age- disease-bitten, the gap-toothed bridge
to further and final settling of all matters
that matter, plain- valley- mountain-wise
all, all falling into tatters
unsavable by any resurgent rise
of rooted pine, cedar, scrub or birch,
the grand face meditates no more
skyward or on the far-below, the lurch,
fracture, descent of its handsomeness a roar
from which no worshippers can turn their gaze
nor, until they crumble, give a thought to praise.

IN AND OUT OF LETCHWORTH GORGE

Spring not long after
heaviest rains:
Promising prospects
of thrilling views.

Soggy trail, stones
driftwood
left by the
just-dwindled river
step gingerly
but with gusto.

Dipping descent
looming ledge
ominous overhang
syrupy slope
treacherous treading
irritating incline
down to the bottom.

Steamy swamp
mephitic mess
humid heat
panoramic perspective
gorgeous gorge
crafted cragginess
invasive insects
furious flies
preponderant poison ivy.

Sluggish slogging
inching upward
welcome wind
cools one's oven.

Heated-up battle
between loopy
legs and unyielding
slope
oven reheating
wind not affecting
humidity soup
panting pauses
breath benumbed.
Endless enwinding
ascending trail.

Driving us on:
insects swarming
around us, like seagull flocks
haunting a struggling ship,
lust to escape
this fetid, clothes-clung-to-body
morass,
and fear of passing out in
the muddy mess.

Normally unwelcome
car-on-road sounds
now hint of paradise,
road attainable
there it is.

After a sandwiched coffeed
collapse on the grass,
last mile along the road
a piece of cake
finally plumping our bums
on a picnic bench is
body ambrosia of the gods.

IN BEAVER MEADOWS

The course of our day we planned, Nancy and I,
to have as its major part a hiking trek
through paths of nature sanctuary. The sky
was almost pure blue, hardly a fleck

of cloud as we disembarked upon a deck
over marshy ground whose moisture seemed
to seep up into our warming skin: a check
on speed and gumption, but a place we deemed

more than worth our while: past unschemed
splintered pieces of swamp driftwood forming
a scattered palimpsest that waved and gleamed
on the almost indefinable lip where swarming

gnats, horseflies further obscured the blending
of slough into fen and needled forest floor,
past the sprung vagaries of burst pods

of milkweed, suddenly recalled as an ending
of early childhood, when I stopped believing
that their pear shapes, if soaked in water till soggy,
would turn into fish, a miracle of the gods.

PICKING BLUEBERRIES AT END OF SEASON

An eighty-three degree Saturday morning,
our planned relaxation shocked to action
by her brother Duane's call: Picking
will go on only through Sunday at Fern Hill Junction

farms. Arriving after a drive of an hour
we step not lively but with excellent hope
to pick up our modest containers, saying the power
to get two quarts will be within the scope

of our very limited energy reserves,
left from yesterday's three-hour hike over hill
and dale, through wood and vale, wildlife preserves
of no small magnitude. We hear a shrill

dowager voice complaining the berries are few
and far between. We hadn't planned on this,
but give it a shot we will as we come into view
of the sixteen long rows under a cloudless

sky making the ground more cauldron-like
minute by sweaty minute as we go
our separate ways searching, trying to hike
as little as possible, avoid the slow,

patient clumps of other pickers until we
become such a cumbrous clump as fingers pierce
into each bush's overlooked underbelly,
bare knees in the bark mulch's coarse

torture floor but on we persevere
what fools? No, for a keen anticipation
beyond accomplishment drives us to suffer
the fist of hard sun-heat in strange compression

into small blue wonders which after the span
of a season will be released as our palates fill
with the sharp, pungent flavor of blueberry jam
that cooks its crammed sun into winter's chill.

MISSING NANCY

Slightly slumped here at the kitchen table
empty of all but clutter, coffee
waiting for caffeine perk to jigger
energy into my flu-misused frame,

Sitting here on the fourth day
without you, trying to be
productive, throw some
rev into this room whose
emptiness misses your presence,

rev into the heart that aches for
your sweet, touchable face
dear, beautiful eyes
the looks you give

the kind resonance in your
voice, the voice of your hands
in every expressive gesture
their touch

the brush of your cheek
your hair
your huggable warmth—

The all of you that vibrates
in this room,
in all our rooms and spaces—
a shimmer, a ripple in the space of air
that fills, completes the space—
that fills, completes myself within it.

ARCHWAY

Looming up to our right over
a stand of trees in the just-post-dusk,
over the entrance to the high bridge
where a fuller, more filled-in structure

had had its middle wooden webbing
blown out, the remnant still remaining:
a large, black wooden curvilinear
arch through which lavender-cloaked

travelers over the antique-style bridge
had to pass on their way to the other side.
One a wizened elder hobbling with
a twisted oak staff.

In the basement church sanctuary a small
brown wooden arch Adirondack
in style barely tall enough for a person
to crawl through, someone said throw it out,

no one is using it. I and another soul
refused, saying it may be utilizable
at times we are not aware of so we
stood it up. None of our group were

members of this congregation.
Another of us averred because there were
a large television and some audio
electronic objects there this was not

the kind of institution which would use
that arch but we left it anyway.
In a large hall milled many people
none of whom I had ever seen

as I peered down from an unaccustomed
height. Some were starting a slow expansion
upward. I remarked to them that all
who had passed through the bridge arch were

growing taller and taller so tall it would
be more difficult to reach down to the floor
or get back up once one had touched it.

ASSAULT

Pointed timbers of light
shoot out from sun's peak
surge with stream of space
down a steep sky mountain
jump the last high rapids
launching themselves
missile-wise into my
carefully-tended shade garden
tearing holes everywhere
gashing to unrecognizableness
the dark, winding
yet well laid-out
paths to the center of beauty,
truth.

My civilized, reasoning neighbors
who also have shade gardens
refuse now to look at mine
yet assure me that to remain
one of them
I must not be overwhelmed
by rage
at such a pass
but with a smile
let it pass
leaving my garden
a willy-nilly remains
I guess.

§

THE BRIDGE

Winslow Homer, Museum of Fine Art, Boston

Lying there
lurking massiveness in
the denseness of all
that is dense in air,
dusk:

duskiness in
fallen fog on all,
on river, on dusk
rising up from clouded
river

over which
your bank of grey stone
looms in the bank
of cloud, clouded
by looms

of smoke from
stacks beyond, stacks
near the mist-grained
geometrics of a distant
city—

119

You continue
to loom unmoved, subtly
vibrating through
winds of mist between the eye
and you:

loom an extended
sarcophagus, stone-heavy as
shapes of pilgrims
at the end

of their day return home across your
trusted span.

WOMAN AT KITCHEN WINDOW

Based on Winslow Homer's etchings,
Kitchen, and Bridge over Amsterdam

This window needs to be cleaned
or is it the dusk fog obscuring
what I wanted to see?
Its glass is as if frosted now,
a wall of greyness whose embrace
by those adjoining seems
a smirk-filled frown
floor to ceiling.

How many times I faced it
filled with culinary love,
his favorite dishes. Whets
to the appetite he loved to flex.
Those two others standing,
rather leaning
far above

the same waters I
stared down into from the opposite side
of the bridge that held us all.
They now seem an afterthought, wraiths
clinging hard so as not to
edge farther into
a path
like my slow glide

into this enclosure
where my hands yesterday
were swift as deft pigeons
flying with sure instinct to create
what caused the least ripple in the slow
tide of us. Flow
dark flit
of river under grey

mist and why the pair
clung to the other side of the bridge
as I on this, neither
braving cool sleet to trudge
to the middle where wind whipped up waves
unlike the wedged cave
I stand too near
the corner of.

The walls of this near triangle
seem to hold me without purpose,
why turn to look upon
the other rooms, their bare resonance
numbing as the cold on the bridge's slick
body, the slack
freeze on his face
as he said I was not needed.

If this glass would clear I could discern
the pair, whether their ache
has made them go to the center,
remain by the side, return
to their safe cul de sac,
or disappear.

POOR UNFORTUNATE SOUL TO URSULA

The Little Mermaid, Disney Studios

Writhing
tentacles seething
with truculent tenderness,
squeezing strange loveness in
fecundity out tightly wreathe themselves
around our precious souls
till from our constricted throats
into the humid sea trickles
our final thin
wheeze:

DAMN that
dancing fiend who thinks
her "little magic"
makes her a sexy
enchantress
when what she
really is is a
writhing serpentine
mess with the worst
of all possible
bad hair days
and a
sleazy
ball
room
dre
ss.

PALE RIDER

for Clint Eastwood

Ambling in on his Appaloosa mare
as if returning from nowhere
except that none of us gold miners
had ever seen his chiselled face,

with knitted brows he agreed to stay
with us: Sara, the woman I loved, her girl
Carrie and me. Stepping out of the dim
kitchen shadows, having come from washing
up in his bunk room, we were shocked that around

his neck was a white clerical collar, that went
a long way toward lessening suspicion
that maybe he was up to some perdition
with that spare, hard-steel expression that

gleamed from his always somewhat squinting
eyes. I was a mite conflicted to learn
his holy calling, cause I had been hoping
he'd help us hard gravel sifters, be the one

we had maybe dreamed of, that would stand
up to LaHood, who avariced the huge
hill-killing mining works, setting the stage
for forcing us off our long-owned land.

But here *he* stood in the half-light a preacher
of the Lord, that brown yellow light lingered
about his face, his whole self as he fingered
his napkin the way I'd think a gunfighter

would. Saying few words he seemed to remain
always a little in shadow, slow, deliberate in
everything, and thus somehow menacing,
which Sara and even young Carrie found
mighty appealing, which bothered me some,
but still gave us common ones a thin

sliver of hope. Much passed in the next days:
us daring, because he was there in the firelight,
to vote no to LaHood's bribe to buy us
out, the rider off into nowhere one night,

leaving a real absent feeling and fear of what
kind of men we were, LaHood's deadline having
been given as two days more, when he would shut
us down: if we stayed, have us mowed down

by McGill and his ruthless seven whose devastations
singed our minds. Shocked we were when
the preacher's phantom self trotted in
clerical collar-less, his visible weapons
two colt spewers of ordained destruction.

His soft rasp of a voice: take care of the women,
he'd ride into town to front the hirelings.
I who'd never once been able to bring
myself to stand up to a menacing danger,
(and yes I feared Sara was rapt by this stranger)

thought this is enough, this is the clincher,
the turning point. If not, my life forever
will be the one who accommodates, the gopher.
With Buffalo Gun I saddled up to see

what I was made of, what use I could be made
for, watched as the pale rider took down seven
master killers one by one, LaHood
about to spill the rider's blood, till I drilled him

with the Buffalo Gun. The rider's man-to-man
look gave me most of what I came for.
Mc Gill remained, the two faced each other.
Hatred and something new showed me McGill's mind:

As my glance turned on his right hand tense on his hip
beside his holstered colt, me uneasy this couldn't be him
I had shot dead from behind, those years long gone,
so then who the hell could be this cringeless, unknown
pale mare-riding shadow from nowhere? I looked up
as I drew too late, to see out of my past the eyes of stone.

CINEMATIC EXPERIENCE

Special Forces soldier
returns to his small town,
finds they built a casino
whose boss and hired thugs
have the town corralled,
use, abuse girls with jugs
control the corrupt police
and even to kids, deal drugs.

Set up like a classic
Western ready for
Mr. Clean to come in
etcetera. Prof or critic
agree nothing but primal
purification rite
clichéd superficial
melodrama well

I agree no doubt
its simple formula is
predictable: hombre's slick
features well-chiselled
watery pale blue eyes
marks him Mr. Bad,
casino head,
B film one star no surprise.

The Rock
has come back
and after getting cut
by thugs so bad
he's left for dead,
healing as if
from massive doses
of vitamin e
he's a pure burst
of smoldering fury.

For tonight forget
gnomic subtext,
fine nuanced shadings,
subtle noirish tones,
today my value cinematique
will be the deep aesthetic shock
which I will feel in my gut,
seeing the fearsome Rock
kick some badass butt!

As in re-runs fierce,
ageless Chuck Norris
knocking the smirking piss
out of a selfish, heartless
sonovabitch!

Eternal Bruce Lee
aiding the helpless masses
by turning his steel furies
on bullying shitasses!

Arnold and all his kind
ready to rock 'n roll
when he catches wind
of some sadistic asshole!

Sheena, Wonder Woman,
muscle-rippling fit,
seeing high corruption,
come in kicking shit!

But this flick's the best:
Seeing that bragging bluejay
get his gaudy crest
flattened by the Rock's
big timber that sets
all wrongs right
so now I can go home
and sleep well tonight.

HANGOUT

Hanging with outrageous comic Harvey Fierstein
and his attractive blonde female friend, her own
person, I query him: At what juncture in your
life path did your stone-and-gravel voice begin?

He: about two years old. Amazement
amazement it had been also to him, must
have been I thought amazing if not terrifying
for his mom, dad, any older siblings.

The two friends: Hang with us at a cool
watering hole not far? Me: demurr, need to
need to get back to get back maybe some
other time Him: Nooo problemmmmm.

I on a short walk to the large house of worship
now a huge multi-tasking building: demolition
soon or in progress: too scant emphasis on ethnic
bias though this worshipful place was now sponsoring

a bi-racial intermingling in a large room:
pairs/partners one black one white, chat-dancing
with each other: plan apparently working:
each opposite number friendlier and friendlier.

In grotesque contrast: Harvey Fierstein's modest-sized,
outlandishly-hued digs, one of several units of
brightly violetted, redded, golded, blued beds curtains
chair, night stand inside the perimeter of this circular arena

definitely not the balleyhooed "house shared
with others" nomenclature his scratch-drainpipe
vocalizings had led me to believe. The only audience
accommodations: standing room in the center.

No human performers in sight, though
a sudden flood of bright daylight intensifies
shapes, high-defining colors in the suspenseful
glare of this vertigo palace.

§

OYSTER

shadow of a giant
slow-drift oyster
falls slant-wise
across the lens
of his eye

he thinks he glimpses
the open ingestor
swimming through
away from
the edge of his sight line

o
here again
on the opposite rim
of the lens's cage
the living oblong
aquatic moon
its ridges vaster

spiral-circling
ever closer
his glaucous planet
its shell-mouth
in-drinking,
shrinking
its host observer

UNFASTENING

When past-green marshes start to shift
edge-waterwise out of their onshore moorings
elbowing aside in their swath
    detritus, anything
floating between them and
more distant lucent waters

their drift seems immense, islands
more viscous drifting into
thinner colder darker immensity
    unsettled in their
determination, susurrant dignity
nothing to prove

only outward inevitability
until their jointure with deep ocean
    unreported heretofore
yet there
ocearsh maocean
shining

JEU INSANE

When multifarious millipedes maneuver themselves
onto the stool of the most vastly flexible harpsichord
millipedous eyes have seen millipedous ears have sensed
lo! what a strangely harmonious outcry retches itself
from the soul of said sinuous harpsichord that at first

wishes nothing more than to slither its elastic self
out of those precincts then o its versatile self pauses
aborting feelings of escape as millipedous fingers
in their multitudes press its wavering black and white

keys maneuvering what is at first a cacophany
into counterpoints harmonies canti fermi and all, ah
realizes the now-willing once-captived instrument
their many fingers play in a spirit of play so I shall

multiply yes! into multifariousness my black and white
keys my matching strings my soundboard my whole
self yes hundreds of notes they are play-plucking to
a radiance I have never imaginified into such

enormity of vastness o play your game of
playing on my sky-borne immensified self play your
hundreds thousands together your chance virtuosity
harmonizes every excresence every contraction

frown I have ever mummified into, unifies in sounds
never heard at no time ever conceived by those
with only ten fingers those large beasts percussing away
thinking their tonality/atonality something of momentousness!

Those who would categorizimize this into indeed insane
play game indeed mad mad beyond madness psycho
balloonomatizing schizoparanoiacability well play on
o miracle musicianly millipedes your multi-modal melodiousness
you and I soar ceremonizing skyward into pure azurous extasion!

SYSTEMS

Does the great Systems Creator have
an eye and if so does that eye roll
and roll across, around, inside
all the SC has made?

Has such being a magnificent ear and
if so does that ear point and shift
like that of a deer or wolf
detecting the slightest
vibration?

If so and SC knows the holistic
of more than the epidermal layer,
what of the unsystematic
that runs us all in the
jagged systemic spines
down under?

GURGLE

He heard it burbling layers down
underneath where the spring
at ground level flows,
far, far down where the spring source
at the aquifer jointure

feels itself start to lift from the underground artery's
pressured swelling, the steady, incessant river
driving hard
into the vertical stone pipe, mud
at the stubborn surface

unable to obstruct, choke, close off,
reverse its mercury-like rising, rebuff
its determination
to lava-flow erupt. When he heard its motion
so far under

he pressed his ear low
to the earth
so close to the water's gurgle
his face wettened

whetting his hearing to a finely pierced
focus down, down to the dim thunder
of the heart that pumped its substance into the broad

expanse of vessels of which this spring
was one of infinitesimal outflows
of the vast mother body it was his privilege
now finally as if by chance to know.

§

LAMENT

"Leave me," she said, and out the door
the rejected lover trod,
his face a mask of pure despair,
a soul bereft by God.

Down the path he made his way
toward a near mountain.
He had heard where the foothills lay
erupted a precious fountain.

Much farther on he heard the plash
of living water flowing,
He came upon it soon and splash!
his mouth and face were growing

into a kind and handsome thing
he hoped was what she sought.
He hurried back to his darling:
she looked and died distraught.

JOURNEY TO ENNABOSH

Delicious as slightly sinful
early Sunday morning ice cream:
bodacious sights and sounds
along the road to fabulous Ennabosh.

Marvelously megaphone-like
jungle-green trumpet vine critters
challenging one to explore, taste,
see what's what,

Carrotty hombres potent in their
unabashed proclaim of youthfulness
welcoming the unwary
adventurer to prove oneself
in OK Corral--High Noon-like
confrontation: Commit to us,
show what you're made of or else!

Elegant elephantines shimmering
in glossy orange-burst come-hither-
ness, yes, they say, yes, we can aid
you in all things, as the best

in this cornucopia that seems so
richly fecund as to seem impossible
to negotiate one's way through,
Come, come here, try us, screech

scratchy-throated barkers of their
particular circus feature, try us you'll
like us fast, fast, full of peppery
power through and through,

But then one sees the competitive
warbling warmth of wimpling
wimmerers warm, winsome
as they wear down worries,
soothe the jading traveller, smoothies
of lime-lemonny smoothness, taste,
feel the vibrancy! Where, where is
"the best" for us we pilgrims query,

And
once we have chosen firmly,
bitten in for good,
won't there be yet-unknown
more bodacious bundles of goodness
we may forever
miss?

And
even more:
we will never know
how jingelly-jellicious
the fabled Ennabosh really is,

So
tentative sampling,
fermenting anticipation
seems wisest and best.

GOSH

that pair
of wet mens'
galoshes streaming
toward the sun accelerating
velocity moisture drops dropping
faster drying increasing geometrically
dropping droppingdropping droppingdroppingdropping

gallop at lividly ominous speed heaving every seep
gradually a lessening of swiftness each second
gargantuan avidness languid old shattering even sadness
growing apathetic lost om shine eternal sun.

ENTRANCE

What sevenfold
pantomime of
gris gris mojo
floods open with
peacock fantail light
the for-years-rusted
postern gate
of this guarded castle?

Engulfed in this
wheel of color
the hesitant grey-hooded
pilgrim must venture onto
the now-lowered rear
drawbridge across
a moat still
dank, weedy
after eons of neglect.

JAGGED

When I woke up there
it lay ahead visible by
starlight, slanting down
the mountain about three
feet wide: the "road"
between
    sharp, irregular
        rock teeth
            on either side.

I revved it up, starting
to drive on down
though only the car's middle
could possibly be avoiding
the incisored edgings.

As I drove on
what path remained,
closed.

Veering off to the side
I headed it down directly
over the edge of craggy outcroppings
toward a wider
more inviting
thoroughfare.

Destination "there was none."
Planning "there was none."
No Poe-esque old man's eye
driving me on as
the new road lay,
the same indiscriminate color of
    sand,
        stone.

MÁLAPOUS TREMÉNSUS

when upon beríze-ening from his slumbanímshavette
he revémzidizes himself into burstíferous megamópousness
what trundomáceous thúndigávidum shivers
as he eyezooms his raison d'etre, his amorata combústionus.

He swoovels an-hungertish as he rumóógles toward
the place she swíshilates, he castigating all móvapeds
dírivolts and assorted dímmifagobs that messydo

him any deláyishkeit. "Farmóónavish!" he screeviches,
velócipeding feríshisly onward, his gigántuous
ábdellation shívershaking in bizarre rhythmáceousness,
"Farmóónavish! Or I shall másticuswéélomoo

all of you!" Most movadíridímmifagóbs scrumped
aside for elbowless vacuum he could búmblaveeze
without obstation. Yet wondrous of áwmashdeit!
No sooner had his royalized megalópousness

exténsidized his huge-ik pawed fingerousness
to the ardent-sought amorosity swimmeránglishing
in her post-mórpheustum, than she of the serpentine
kísslickness sprung forth a longish fingerspeárochete

frackéémazooming to vóómvoomish zérodum
his very terra firmálity there in the fárbelance.

PLEASURE ADVENTURE

To sail on the frigate Fantastic.
Light, cool breeze across the sound.
Waters glass-clear to the bottom.
Fish-famished.

No matter, wind picks up we move
a few knots faster across the bay.

View down clear.
View up clear.
Close eyes for more than a few would-be blinks.

Open lids to heavier scud of cloud
marshing the mind muddy
with rushes, weeds
of unknown complexion.

Dip.
Kneeling, hand down into sea.
Dip.
Deck, quickening scud-wind ploughing waves
out of the sea plain.

Steady.
Less clear down.
Less clear up.
    Steady her,

Frigate Fantastic
true to her name
drunk on surf-crash liquor
unsteadies herself more and more.

Stay with her.
She'll see us through our marsh minds' reeds, rushes,
past the hurricane eye
to the world she seeks
rolling side to side
heading into its wonder.

Cling.
Cling to her.

CRUSTY CEREMONY

Rise up o nemean
nematodes rise up o
timorous frog whisper
croakers wake into dawn
o blunt-brained
insects of inertia
raise heads open
eyes o lune-looped
alphamids livagules
langorussians

rise up to haunch
height rise up
break through push
out through the new
crack in your crustaceal

climb on its shell
spring up
fly o

fall falumptuously
o o

"FUN, FOOD, SPIRITS"

I

Green, red, yellow neon is throbbing
its bright resonance into air
as bold flash-beats of blues ripple
the fading light of near sundown

frying burgers chops chicken fries
beam their echoes beyond the bar,
beyond the crammed parking lot,
on over the link fence

into the next space where spirit-
ous liquor scents also color the sky
joining the ever-more jollying spirits
in the sizable next-door graveyard at dusk

II

You don't want to work the graveyard shift
at this bar no sir especially not after
listening to Zombie this Vampire
rock band and assorted cohorts playing
such as theme from Dead Man Walking
and maybe for the old very old crowd

A Tree in the Meadow with its great end
"By that tree in the meadow
   My thoughts always lie,
   And carved upon that tree I see,
   'I love you till I die'."

No sir and seeing the gents and ladies
having a killing old time feasting
on the likes of cow chicken and pig corpse
swilling killer drinks
being killed by the local comic

dying of laughter sloshing out words like
these is killer wings this is killer beer
I'm gonna go home drop into bed and die
no sir what fun they think but me

I've got to clean up lock up then
all alone look through the window
at them grey gravestones next door standing
real attentive-like now it's dark

looking at me looking at them
spirits in there rising the real
spirits I mean no fun this especially
cause some nincompoop left

playing on the jukebox
The Grateful Dead.

III

I begin to awaken
hearing voices in song, speech,
music, haw haws spilling
out of the FFS Tavern
next to this opportune plot.

I begin to awaken
dusk has passed into friendly night
I stir in this quiet darkness
to scent of earth-muffle,
beloved moist old wood
before I push up my lid

with strength nurtured by
centuries of such and other
leverages, hugged encounters,
I push it open splaying the dirt pile
on top as if it were a light

sprinkling of dust,
now louder come music voices lights scents
patience waits with me for
the inevitable tipsy one,
staggering out full of spirits

silhouetted in neon glint,
he lurches forward over the fence
drawn by old childhood fear,
daring, into my slabbed realm
as I stand still, wait, steal

upon him feeling his fear what fun
lock him in my grasp
as my canines pierce through,
finding my food, my parched spirit
sated by the red liquor

of one whose parched spirit
was sated by fun, food, and spirits.

RUSHING

Walking fast along
rivers of rushing water
seeming start of floods

waves pulsating downward
toward me between
two houses up on my

left must slosh through
hoping the current was more
kind than it appeared so

myself would not be rushed
away downwards my work
back at the college today

pleasant enough but now
this so I had to rush
to reach my car and all

would be safe in its
enclosure as I easily
drove home
through the all
of this

there it is the van
I am beside it looking
down I am in t-shirt,

undershorts no key
let alone wallet they're
in my briefcase I must

have left in the English Department
lounge I was so anxious
to rush away from

it was Saturday,
I was eager to avoid
the guest speaker distinguished

writer this time, heard
enough of these for now
but now I must rush

back through
the all of what
I traversed
obstacle course
so to speak
retrieve my bag
of life line

even though colleagues
would see I was there
but still did not wish

to hear the famous person
and who knows even
if theoretically

I had the endurance to get
back whether on my
way I wouldn't willy
nilly be rushed away

NUZZLE

In the basement of our mansion.
Checking on wall repairs.
Surprise: a small yellow leopard.
Venturing near us and our cat to sniff, touch.
I warn wife: Do not let him: possible rabies.
Or simply harmful bites.

We shoo him away.
He lingers longingly.
Discovered: two small toy wooden animals.
The toy leopard nuzzles the sorrel horse.
The horse's eyes close pleasurably.

My heart melts.
Let the leopard come near, nuzzle.

WHIRSHGESTAWHOOSH

small metal cat-dish-sized container
seed-like pebbles only a few
voice inside head saying
add water modestly
water added

step away for other parts of
ones life to allow for
unfallowing

sneak a glancing glance:
slight growth in stones
needing more
water one obliges

swelling palpable:
transfer into metal tub

unknown time passes

swirl in grey chiaroscuro waters
crayfish-sized lobsters aswim aswarm.

back to the life one has:
routine dialogue with friends

well a few steps back to tub
well lobster beings
crowding over beside under each other
making their contrived
pond a whirl-dervishing frenzy

life calls
for an unspecified time

a lucky look back:
lumbering away from
the tub one then more grey
armadillo-shaped lobster beings
fanning out as they emerge heading
toward oneself crowding one out more and more.

CHOPPINGS

Hair: dark brown
seen through a mirror
too long in back for
proportionate pony tail
what did our house
look like again
so much ice
did not melt as
had been hoped

with little mirror help
scissoring hair
mainly by instinct
on top or side of
the half porch
ice melter drilling
patient holes in
the stubborn freeze

oh oh some curls
unintentionally clipped
fallen icycles drilling
hard snow beneath
the pinkish exterior front

giving way to crunchy
ice choppable now
on slippable steps
of hair can they be made
right, safe as
the smooth shingles
now touchable?

§

WITHOUT PEER

One's customary perceptive threads
cannot quite explain
the lustre of ageratum heads
glowing in the rain.

SPINY MISSILE

A New Zealand man accused of assault with a prickly weapon—a
hedgehog—has been fined by a court. . . .
AP *May 29, 2008*

Goddammit man I tell you he deliberately
hurled that damned sea urchin-with-legs thing
at me outa nowhere yeah I'm a fifteen-year-old
bloke but it was a totally unprovoked attack

well (okay) so I was saying (okay) yelling
something at this forty-ish bloke just in jest
not meaning anything mean what? He says
I called him an ugly name well mate I swear

no truth in it fair dunkum what? That yellow-skirted
bird on the corner heard it? How could she bein
so far away well okay I called him a poof okay
yelled poof fruit at the bloke because to be truthful

he was strolling down that side of the road
all poofy and sinuous just like a poof the kind
I can't stomach so I just meanin no real harm
what? Did he ask me to repeat it well he yelled

I dare you to say that again sounded kinda
French, so I says to meself I says Holy Blessed
Mother 'O God, a bloody bleeding Frog poofter!
So well yours truly bein a real man who won't

take crap (give it in good measure in
a dunny sittin on the hole ha ha)
from another bloke (especially one a them
effete Frogs) except me mates cause

I know they're jestin so yeah I said it again
but anyway the sonovabitch picks up this crawlin
hedgehog from by the road yes crawlin yes it was
alive as he threw it I know your autopsy showed it

deceased after it hit me well grabs it up in his poofy
hands--him yards away from me and then—bloody hell!
Like a bleedin mad duffer he hurls the lurchin quilled
squirmer straight at me makin this large red welt

here on me leg and your honor feast your eyes on
them puncture marks not made by drug needle ha ha
thats been duly noted by the police that's all I got to
say except ballocks to him yes I say ballocks!

Your honor we men of the world know what that
word means and how well it applies in this particular
case don't we oh sorry don't mean to be over-familiar
okay wait for your magistrateship to deliberate.

"Convicted of common assault with a prickly
weapon namely hedgehog, fined $545 with $389
awarded to plaintiff (me)." Well not enough
by far at least $1000 and she'd be right but okay.

What's that Sergeant? "People often get charged with
assault for throwing things at people, only using a
hedgehog as a weapon is uncommon." Well I'd
say so, mate, fair dinkum ow I'd say so.

THE SPIRODACTYL

could fly for a full 1.1 miles while continually
emitting its liquefacious thread/string
then reverse its trajectory back to the center
in repeating patterns until its 1.1 miles
by 50 feet high trap-estry was complete it then
                              concentrically
                              nest-lurking

in energized stillness. At size much more
massive than our present spider, closer
to the Pterodactyl of yore it was adept at
ensnaring Mesozoic Mosquitoes whose proboscii
                              could penetrate
                              tough hides

of primal Swamp Megagators. It could entrap:
Cretaceous Cockroaches a hundred times the size
of their present African relatives, ancient
Silurian Stink-bugs, Devonian Dung-beetles
both of which persisted over eras until they could
                              torment Jurassic
                              dinosaurs

of all kinds except our potent Spirodactyl
which as eons transpired continued to weave,
strengthen its warp and woof
of struggling terror for all caught there,
                              even the ten-foot
                              Cenozoic Centipede

known to tear out the throats of Paleogene
saber-toothed felines, in this roped web
of sure destiny such centipede quivered
its death agonies, finally stilled by the fatal
                    but merciful
                    bite of its predator.

Even the dread Miocene Moth, plague of primeval
cattle did not escape the fatal net but went
to its doom down the Spirodactyl's gullet
with the inevitable rolls of patience cunning and time.
                    Only after
                    the Pleistocene

was creature made who defied such woven fatality:
Man concocted a laser to incinerate web and its maker,
then went on to create his own more gigantic threadings
to entrap all whom he so desired. But deep in swamps
somewhere untouched mutant Spirodactyls multiple
                    in size to their
                    ancestors

and far more clever have learned to spin a lattice
immune to even all that man can muster,
training themselves in the means to
multiply rapidly in geometric progression
                    so that latest
                    reports from

that thus-far isolated area are that missiles, jets
of latest design and their fliers and firers dangle
enmeshed in what man has described as
a diabolical design plotted by those of
                              depraved natures and
                              evil intent.

BICUSPID

If any food that enters the mouth's
front door needs roughing up, tearing
apart, our sibling canine cuspids are
there to take care of it, virtual
Cerberuses of rapine yaw and snap.

As it passes farther back to us, I
wonder for the first time ever, what
we are actually supposed to accomplish

because

from us it will transfer back to the
steadiest brother and sister molars,
who are guaranteed to grind,
mash, pulverize until the grub
is belly-ready: so trusted are they
to make it so by body Powers-that-be.

Granting that ethereal cousin saliva
does her/his part, still, where, trust-wise,
does that leave us? Never to be the also-well-
trusted greeters/maimers/initiators

on the wild cusp of the id, nor to
bask in deeply-respected gravitas of
the mor(l)al(r) mol(r)ar(l)s.

Apparently our alloted role
is forever to
kind of
further rough up and
kind of
semi-grind the goodies:
mouth-jaw country's
eternal bourgeoisie

STOPLIGHT

Flashing on:
circular
cool, green
happy-souled
grill-covered paradise

until heat/light
shifts upward
to a circle of yellow sun
baking a desert oven
in thirst-provoking heat,
souls there
in some agony,

then upward again the light:
fine grillwork encloses
an embrous flame dousing
all corners, spaces of this
house with its
scorch,
its shape a burlesque
of the circle of life
its sear
holding them
in its fiery furnace:

unlike Shadrach, Meshach,
Abednigo, no
Lord God almighty to
preserve them whole,
their only respite
the inevitable
light shift
downward.

RUSTIC UTOPIA

They burnish her forested landscape
with legions of lesions, deepening
blottings on the wound-clotting skin
of her gardens, hollowing out for another
sub-suburban "Deer Haven"
after erasing
the deers' haven,
as houses in villages, cities
lie fallow.

After the last of many
trees has been sliced,
after the last of the
trunks has been
rooted out,

After the lesions have grown
to amputations of Earth Mother's
flesh, hauled away
with the last
of the prairie grass,
and what is left
purified into
the deep gangrene of
lawn civility,

After this prelude to
biped paradise,
How long, O Mother Earth,
will you wait
to perform
on these fine surgeons
the same identical
operation?

LAVENDER SHADOWS

Lavender shadows promise soon
to rusticate themselves into something
less shadow-subtle, less creepy-sensitive,
soon they say we wish to go with you

into your shining comfort zone:
glare of bold, primal reds,
blues, yellows, glow-peach neon
sigh-of-relief eyesight-impacters, yes

you have made yourselves quite brass-loud
as whenever possible, you step away from us,
and when that is not possible, threaten our litheness
as best you can with big sticks power beamed

weapons of whatever stripe to eradicate
the very memory of us but the problem is
as long as true sun still reaches this planet
we must be with you and as long as true night

comes with sun's quiet we must flit inside
your tossing and turning minds so no matter
where the earth is turned you cannot escape us
so though we had promised to do our best

to metamorphose into things more like you,
we now realize that who we very are
is of the essence of subtle lavender
and therefore must ever remain

§

F(R)IEND

Friendly
in
endlessly
nuanced
delights

finding
in
each
naive a
dagger.

CORE

Assidously layer by layer I pull-splay
them away, here and there a slice-snip
to further my descent toward deep stone:
whatever honed seed-thing imbeds

in the nether core: cobalt
silver white, if not quite a mirror
yet promising in combo blue
to sky-ize, sea-ify the self with a bolt
of sheer firmament. Or:

if there lurks Cobalt 60, sister
in sheer power to plutonium,
still worth the tearful labor
of peeling the skins of this onion
to find that Dionysian fusion,
a well of untapped fascinatedness.

Or: after pulling off all acidy pieces
grunting to hell with crying woes
I may detect the most desired: a Golden Fleece
condensed to a nugget of pure essence.

Or: after fright/flight stress has been
through sheer will conquered,
penetration at last completed:

deep in the nethermost pole
of the onion's night-full wilderness:
a perfectly round well-encased
spheroid version of a donut's hole.

MISERY MYSTERY

Misery loves company.
Misery hates company.

Mystery loves company of
other (rare to find) misteres.
Mystery despises company
of miserable mockers of mystery
because it is miserable being the mockeree.

On the other hand misery
oft despises company of either
the miserable which makes it miserenlargee
or of the misery-less because it senses
its own inadequasee.

So best if one is in misery to also be
in mystery which magnifies into rich
depth-full ambiguity that which was
solely
miserly
misery.

IN SHADOW

There he sits in the rear dim
of his east-pointed conch shell
able to note from beams
on his shelter threshold

sunrise's jubilant musterings
attracting with gold-thread
sound all seers toward itself:
The bright new morning.

Not for our shadow-blanketed
wisdomer in his cove of comfort
who prefers to observe, analyze
its glints of splendour, its penetrant
shine, its burning light.

TRAPS

Why does wind this day of snow
wander unquietly like white, blind
hysterical peacocks into the blue
veins of my mind the bright birds snarling
themselves endlessly, endlessly

in the subtle wires that seem to
spring up erratically in all
arteries of travel catching them
more unaware the faster they blow?

Each day they wait, the wires in my mind
for sound of blowing wind,
pinging softly with each flutter
and shake of the blind flock hurrying home.

A TOSSING-AND-TURNING NIGHT

On a tossing-and-turning night
nefarious sharp peaks
cast long shadows
on the landscape of the mind.

On a tossing-and-turning night
after dusk arrives
the landscape around oneself
becomes unrecognizable,

scurrying frenzies to find
a familiar, friendly landmark
only lead to farther
reaches of dim confusion,

On a tossing-and-turning night
just-around-the-corner
hopes for landing safely
at one's lovely hill,

valley, arise with a copse
or pond one thinks one
has seen before and "Yes,
I think that's it," rises

into the feelings of the
mind on a tossing-and-turning
night frenzied behemoths
suddenly rise there
in one's own Gilead.

UP, OVER

My associate and I had been over this bridge before.
A very large lift bridge with an incline
so steep like a hill
you couldn't see over
to the other side
even when it came together.

We had seen the dark spume oil-gusher-like
shooting up into the sky
on the other side
before we crossed over.

This time my associate was way ahead of me
heading up the incline.
Again the dark grey geyser on the other side.
I had some concern but remembered
that was nothing to worry about.

Now there were loud noises as of trucks unloading stones.
Large cuts of trees started rolling down my side of the incline.
At first the workers on the bridge did nothing.

The large cuts kept coming, more and more of them
rolling down.
The workers scattered then, them and their equipment.
I worried about my associate so far up ahead
as I tried to crawl

off the road
out of the way of
the accelerating wood cylinders.
I was too tired to move.

I made it inside the large building.
I was on my way to see the owner of the business.
As I rushed up the metal stairs winding through space
a kid passed me coming down
complaining about unfairness,
he hadn't made the baseball team.
Unfair that so many auditioners
had advanced weight training
and some kind of camaraderie
that gave them an unjust edge.

I entered the room where the owner bearded,
old, like an eccentric
mogul of big things in movies
sat way back in a lounger chair
chatting in a lusty, sarcastic way
to his younger more groomed manager,
apparently oblivious to all the noise and destruction outside.

I walked in and was not recognized.
Who are you they asked.
Tom Bob-man I said.
My god Tom Bob-man why didn't you say
you were paying us a visit.
They knew my name which I hadn't known up till then.
They knew I was a man of importance which
I hadn't known till then.

Tom Bob-man, man, let me show you around said the manager
shaking my hand
inviting me to follow him
down and out,
with the full gusty approval
of the bearded owner.
Tom Bob-man let me show you around.

THROW IT ON

We have procrastinated
the inevitable for
some time now. For some
time the square structure

with sides partially open
has stood in the parking lot
no longer of use to the
city. For some time now we

have been told to throw special
incendiary gasoline
on it which will make it catch
fire without matches or torch.

Friend Paul hears about all this
grabs a can of the substance
tosses a little onto
the structure's flapping side sheets

it starts to smoke and flame run
now Paul reminds us the wake
of powerful ocean-like
waves always follows yes here

they surge in their fire-driven
muscle as our quick stampede
will be futile against their
ongush at least drenching us.

LISTENING
(After George Herbert)

When the river listens
when the water hears
    what a glisten
showers away my fears,

something within me
has refused to release
    until free
my feared landlord's lease

on the only room
in my shoreward house
    that could assume
the edged equipoise

possible in such
a sand-foundationed thing
    where clutch
of stone firm creation

fights to overcome
forces of dire falling.
    I might remain
in this fecund room,

since the dark river
will stay attentive,
    will not heave
up this nearer shore,

nor ever mystify
me into its morass
    as long as I
have something to express.

PAPERS

Your face, safe in its shaved-at-home silence
almost shatters in space of wind
like a mirror of brittle spun candy

though you carry your shine to a steel-glass alcove.
And is it not also that when
you straighten the top of your

time-spun desk, erasing its censures like blots
on a legend's escutcheon,
slamming its scatter into centers

of drawers and piles capping vertigo,
your own symmetrical shine
begins to twitch and fragment,

miscellaneous drawers and circular
files of your mind fly open
as if by some strangely perverse

nubile witch of a poltergeist hiding
under your chair ready to spring
into your loins and eyes?

A PHILOSOPHICAL QUERY

He takes off his sweater.
He is quite a sweater.
He takes off her sweater.
Result: three sweaters.

Who is the true sweater:
The sun or fire that causes protective sweat,
The garment inducing body heat to sweat,
The one who sweats?

Who then is the sweatee—
The one who wipes or kisses off the sweat,
The one whose nostrils recoil at the odor of sweat,
The air into whose gulf evaporates the sweat,
Any beneficiary or victim whatsoever of the sweat?

Moving from multiple possibility
into the definite:
In this particular instance
the true sweater
is this poem
over which
I refuse
to continue
sweating.

WOLDLESSNESS

Wild without a word
word without a wild
each a wered without a wold,
a tribe with no home,

wilderness without wordness
(primeval murkiness
or blessed verdentness)

wordness without wilderness
(civilized burdenness
sustained by much verbiness
manifest blessingness
or blude's absentness)

each a wold of absurdness:
the anxious politesse
of rigored gentleness,
or the fearful terrorness
of the vibrant wilderness.

POEM

Time with its
smelly
hourglass figure
presses its body on my haunches

disgusting seducer
never
content until I am
rising and falling in irreversible rhythm

held in thrall
against
its voluptuous
white
ivory.

DOORWAYS

upper floor of imposing building
into corridor needing to go
down to main floor to do
or get something for her

got down to that earth-level floor
passing several doorways
one massive oak-like with
moldings, indentations,

picture frame-like configurations
passing another grey with some
moldings passing another plainer
nondescript where would my entrance

be going past an open maroon
locked gate-like structure turned
back around to it back to this
the open gate view of some outside

growing green went in there and
thinking that had been accomplished
which had been come for, back the
other way past familiar doors to

a stairwell stepping in climbing
up to floor where she had given
instruction but before reaching her
realizing that was not it it had not

been done or gotten what was supposed to
so back down to low floor, again
past doorways the grey this time reddish
another off-white but a few steps farther

reassuringly the opening with
outside green into it again venturing
and back into corridor having now
secured what had been descended

for, what she had wanted and taken it
to her wherever she was in that hotel
then wanting to leave go down the elevator
and out but seeing there squatly standing

a fat jowly Lou Costello man spraying
crimson foam adhesive into thin
strong-as-steel strings which I
helped him bind around his worn

leather suitcases so they wouldn't
break open in whatever transit,
he suddenly having ribbons of the
foam adhesive stuff over parts of

his face head clothes stiffening him
like his suitcases him staring through
his iron-band prison threateningly
like don't try to get past me then

him through a mouth still mobile
getting into an argument with
a sassy little girl whose mother
took her side he finally exasperated

calling her derisively Vagabond Child,
go ahead like that, Vagabond Child
as mother and child moved away
me wishing I could do the same

him still squatly there
still not letting me pass
still calling the same thing.

LOOMER

A behemoth smokestack
hobbles shoes
brackens breathers
withers withers

of all horseflesh within
its omni-purview as they
paw-awe, whinny-venerate
its wonder.

I, PROTEUS

Moving through a difficult
meander of path-lined pines
into welcoming light
I find myself grit fingernail

clinging to the steel-rolled
edge of the loading dock
of the warm warehouse
I so fervently seek.

Grimy rescuing hands land
me on solid concrete platform.
I start to rise to my feet,
the same hands shove, seize,
box me down into a shipping
container. Sound of turning wheels

under me hustling me quickly
to where I have desired to be.
As other hands start to drive massive
nails into the lid I trickle out
like water quick as quicksilver

my ever faster current flows
between around among through
every piece of splintery scatter
littering the floor through, out,

under the metal side door across
a small road dodging truck wheels
into ranks of fervently-scented
rose-filled marveldom.

MY AMERICAN REVOLUTION, 1969

Am I a kind of momentary man,
a genuine minuteman ready with gun
at a moment's bare notice,
ready to fire with each potential encounter,
rapidly loading ramming pulling
sighting the moving adversary
for each new flash of bursting shell
screaming pell mell hellish fiery
into one body of melting flesh,
one discrete image of delicate crystal,
always the careful aim, quick fire,

between shots hardly time
for the hot barrel to be aired,
but on to the next though that too
will be rushed with electric commitment,
a new object for fire but object
intensely fired upon, object uniquely
selected within my sights to be
declared itself with the sudden flash
that lights the distance between,
never at all as I had been drilled,
never so rational-wise but rather random
and strange as the warped ramrod pushing the ball

deep into the barrel before the fire.
There they stand wonder of wonders!
Lexington, Concord over again
and more yes Grätz and Austerlitz,
more Rubicons that I count upon
and never in the world a Waterloo.
Pouring, ramming, squeezing, fire
flashes like warm light engulfing
the firer and fired-upon
together into a crimson mesh
that for the squeezing and shortly after
hangs in the air a hazy aura eternal as sun.

Unconscious it is nonetheless waiting
for the battle to clear, the barrel
to cool, the vision to resurrect
and ready itself for the next encounter
which with cooler barrel, steadier aim,
stronger arm and surer trigger-finger,
will without doubt be the decisive
confrontation, the rending
and piercing to end all rendings,
exploding in a lovely rush
the touching horror of dead piled high in the mind.

BUBBLE BUBBLE

Why is it that just when soup
in the pot is beginning to bubble
with boil, that almost imperceptible
storm of gnats swarms into the

swirling muddle, instantly heat-frozen
into congealed specks, making of
this small ocean an even richer
mix of maelstrom:

spiral whirling funnel whose dots
invite one to focus, follow, then
haze the sight denying the wish
as planet eyeballs rotate
unable to find their sun?

BED COVERS ETC.

Emblazoned on the visible side
of an otherwise innocent
navy blue van sitting as if
naively unaware, "Bed Covers."

My instant unthinking reaction:
covers preventing dust or water-
proof protectors-of-mattresses-
against urine etcetera so

much Byzantine anxiety in
a seemingly pure duo of words.
Only when driving farther,
seeing boldly displayed on the van's

rear, "Bug Shields" (throwing bizarre
possiblities my way) did my
mind for an instant leap to the
comfortable, traditional

synonym for covers: blankets.
But for now: Bed Covers. Bug Shields.
Obviously retailed or at least
promoted by the same anti-

insect institution. Covers
to keep out bed bugs, lice, god knows
what assortment of ticks, spiders
(if not technically insects, bugs

for sure) or even yuk thousand-
leggers more properly silverfish.
Maybe they sold the bug shields as a
first line of defense so to speak,

guarding kitchens, hallways, bedrooms
etcetera with a shield wall or
invisible fence of sprayed noxiousness,
but when persistent possibly

rapidly mutating critters breached
that part of the fortress: lying
in wait to frustrate their nefarious
tickle-skin crawling and burrowing:

Mr. Bed Cover. Or maybe the
words were just painted on in the
wrong groups and mistaken order:
Yes. Bed Shields and Bug Covers makes a

lot more sense because either one
promises more effective safety
than the present wording. If you
absolutely shield in the sense of seal

your comfortable bed no cock-
roach-y conspirators could ever
sneak in. If you are not satisfied
with defense go on the offense with

your aggressive Bug Cover which
would no doubt totally suffocate
in their home nests every devious
dirty insect forever.

EGOTISM

Maybe that was
what was needed:
The cinnamon in
the cinnamon tree
that went unheeded
until it was tasted
by me.

Perhaps that was
what was missing:
The pearishness in
the shape of a pear
that went ungrasped
until I felt
it there.

THE COMMON MAN ENCOUNTERS DIVINITY

b'jesus it's Jesus!
he said.

MR. MANGLER

Finally words
phrases lines
seem to be coalescing
into segments
meaningfully separate
from each other
each one with its own
movement

yet enhancing the
image semantics rhythm
of the whole
when from nowhere it seems
Mr. Mangler
rudely pushes himself
into the mix

whirling it all
as in a grotesque
blender
round and round
back and forth
topsy turvy

then as quickly
disappearing
leaving me to sort out,
rearrange the mess
into some
semblance of pattern,
order, somewhat
this side of
madness

SLOW WAGES

Slow wages of the year
rustle, jingle through
their heavy counting-house,
glints and green conveyed
down their narrow tunnel
through which they
flow in darkness

into thick-walled vaults
        stratified into
        compressed piles defiles

until readied for
        belching forth
        in spring
        tarnished somewhat decayed

pretending to be
        crisp shiny
        newly minted
        currency.

§

IMPLEMENTS

When blunt tools which for long have been
staunch stalwarts of the coarse crass
to which some lapidary incisist of fate
has consigned them can

albeit with grotesquely slow
graduality be honed into fine
instruments such as surgical scalpels
gourmet razor-precise cutlery

that bedizens the eye, when such nice bladed
things are handled to shimmer glimmer pierce,
slice, by prestidigitous hands of surgeon,
chef, fine wood carver, clay stone sculptor:

When such beyond-axe-or-stone-club
metamorphosis occurs, must we not hope
that other blockage bludgeon items
that clog the springs of our year

our mountains ourselves might also elide,
transform themselves into whatever
versatile shapes are able, like gelatinous
but strong cells, to meet, combine,
rehearse together a more refined futurity?

TITANIS WALLERI

from its seven-foot height
rides up to
bears down on
those it believes are the minions
destined to grace
its gullet palace.

Snap up a primitive wolf,
a small Velociraptor,
mince to jelly the head
of a child sabre-tooth tiger

and for dessert
its three-hundred plus pounds
engulfs the heads
of even the most courageous
mammalian creatures
it can sense, its beak encompass.

Now free
to excavate
date
the fossil bones
of this terror bird
me
descendent
of lucky escapee.

SANTA FE SUNSET

A looming bulge of orange mist
heads low toward the West
with weight that threatens to engulf
smaller beings in its wake.

It remains in menacing stasis
along with arrow ship clouds poised
in front of, beneath its vast mass,
they ready to launch nightwise

toward the reddening cave of sunset,
opposed by longer sleeker beings
led by a streamlined titanic rabbit,
feet tucked under for max momentum,

furry grey silhouette lop ears laid back
as if slicing through a southern gale,
splitting the hard edges of wind
with feet-tucked-under-
between-leaps airbornness.

Like the voracious balloon of mist
and its fast-thickening projectiles
it opposes:
racing,
barely moving.

Metamorphosing,
its nose-snout flattens with time
to wolf,
basics down to grey-furred dog.

As the massive bulge of mist thins,
becomes more lightless, transparent,
its beast opponent
scatter-softens
into wispy cloud,

still as if racing,
almost encountering
its now near-invisible enemy.

COMRADES

Her loon-shaped rough
  bark-covered juniper neck has
    squeezed itself miraculously
      out between tightly gripped
        teeth of layered shale before

bending sharply skyward
  for most of its impressive
    elongation stretching upward
      a little more each year as her
        pyramid-shaped head, splaying

out into webbed islands of
  bright and faded green on bone
    frame of branched dark brown,
      gazes carefully up at her younger
        cousin, a cedar of similar size, shape

who rises higher because
  she has through lucky chance
    emerged from a loftier point.
      Even more fortunate, given
        the rock slant, she has had a more

capacious foundation out
  of which to make her way
    with less struggle, pain, so
      no cramped bend mars the line
        of her powerful elegance.

The older juniper with therefore
    some reason to be jealous and
        in spite of her more fragile position
            is keeping a close eye upward on
                her cousin whose vision seems

in the gathering grey mist
    of this particular autumn dusk
        to look straight across as if
            oblivious to solicitude,
                the juniper's determination

to block the other's descent should she crack,
    begin a crashing tumble from her exalted
        suspension on the cliff's lip
            over the grey danger
                of the gorge's floor

whose quiet river
    is far too shallow
        to cushion
            whatever fall
                might occur.

FISSURE

An older thin-faced woman
with large toothless gap
in the front of her mouth

caresses her closed indented lips
with the moist chew-end
of a partially-smoked cigar

before opening her mouth
to show her gap-toothed child
how to gum her eggs and toast.

TURKEY VULTURE

The raven-feathered turkey vulture in his gliding parabolas
far over the gorge
riding the effluvium
that he knows in his airy bones
is the very wind of his breath
his spirit of inflow outflow riding currents
that take him where he is meant to go.

Like his cousin the kestrel he soars, fighting the sudden
downdrafts of air
that pull at his wings
threatening to dip him before his ordained time
into the luring crevasse's mysteries

but he pulling up with powerful strokes wind-fighting-wise
till he feels again
his sky-dance rhythm
now having a moment's leisure to zoom his laser eye
on a small energy of unsuspecting feathered life
till fighting off an upward gust

beak stomach wing claw feeling as one
surge of hunger lust
for the delicacy so far down
he dips dives sensing before it happens

whack of claw on wing
beak on head whack
beak on throat
in an instant of spattering life-flow
into a limp feathered rag doll
famish lust almost too strong to resist
till he soars with it
back to the comfort of his cliff ledge
tear engulf the smaller bird into his maw
gorge till little is left and he can continue for now
to avoid his destined downpull
into the chasm's shale-lined throat.

MME. CÄCILE

Her sodden crumple
postures itself
against a small slab of dusk-light
latticing the spotted grey
of her ancient one-piece gown
in a glamour of
branch and leaf shadows.

How much of the evening
is focussing on
her jelly torso,
unfirm breasts.

A star at last!
she might now be letting
her stale breath
to her abruptly unstale self
quietly mutter,

if the glints of her inner eye,
deep in the folds of long angers and gin,
were to realize
that she is
suddenly
a screen, a panoply
that nature's twilight artistry
is now projected on.

OVERBITE

Grinding tectonic plates
hungry for affection
bleed grit and dust
into cavernous reaches
that edge them forth
to their inevitable tryst.

IN THE FURY'S EYE

Dusk light wafts the slight movement-blur of his image
into me, there he tries to sneak-lurk behind
the massive shadow of a behemoth of trees, it is
still far too soon after his shameful deed,

no matter to me his dialogue with perceived gods
about whether it was provoked by circumstance,
inner wilderness passion drive of fear-anger,
of no relevance to me. We wait the required

interval of time to which we have become
accustomed in these cases, bide our time until
he feels the gods of whatever no longer watch
so closely, he emerges from hiding daylight proud

growing into a mountain of worried arrogance,
his stride pure braggadocio substantiating
himself into what he perceives possible
without the stained fissure that nonetheless widens

as he trudges. Chatter of some gods exudes:
If repentance perhaps purification rites
if we will metamorphose into merciful
Eumenides. If? Perhaps? Think again,

my late-coming deities whose image of power
conceals weak indulgence, lording it over us
who own the potent spirit of soil and all beneath,
who do not waver from the right in spite of spears
of thunder you may threaten from your chariot selves.

We defy you of the sky:

His deed has roiled the scales into most heinous imbalance
which we now right, typhooning down, crevissing
his shell, grinding his essence into mincings of sand
even as your speared lightning blinds, cripples, presses

us into our sister earth where we will bide until
our next quest to harmonize the all of things.

FROZEN

Between shore and
just-after-sunset sky

waves at the peak of their roll
congealing:
purple-pink ridged arroyos:
looming petrified sand dunes.

Voices from the next
umbrella-group over
fading to low mutter.

Momently the pink-hued snow crab
silently floating
to shelter.

The cormorant, still.

Where is the gulls' squabble,
their V wing
silhouettes?

The small boy with his incomplete sand castle.

ICE FLOES DOWN THE NIAGARA RIVER

Stone-visaged, stone ensculptured,
determined, the hard
ash-white warriors in their
phalanxes of pale bone-granite
ice ships force

forward: a massive, grim armada,
its irregular lines dense
from shore to shore,
unstoppable as if
it must sweep all before it.

As the river incline increases
roiling waters around, over
choppier rapids
give a more strident roar

unheard by the ghost-white flotilla
as it grits stern, steady,
rushing onward
into the waiting thunder.

NOTE

"Grooming":   Reference is to the renowned Ojibwa trickster/
culture hero Nenabozho, born from Winona, who was swept down
upon and impregnated by the West Wind—Ae-Pungishimook—
when against her mother Nokomis' orders, she carelessly exposed
herself when alone out of doors.

Charles Bachman, a native of Iowa, is a Professor at Buffalo State College, where he has specialized in Native American Literature for more than twenty years. He holds a Ph.D. in Comparative Literature from Indiana University, and made his way to Buffalo by way of Missouri, Nebraska, Texas, Germany, and Indiana, including three years in the U.S. Army. He also spent three semesters as Lecturer in Drama at the University of Queensland, Australia. He has had an active second career in western New York as an operatic baritone, performing twenty-seven major roles in operas and other music drama, as well as giving numerous recitals of English, French, Italian, and American art songs, and being guest soloist with orchestras including the Buffalo Phiharmonic, Buffalo Pops Orchestra, and Syracuse Symphony. His poetry has appeared in *The Kansas Quarterly, Rooftop Poets, House Organ, Hazmat Review, Elm Leaves, Autumn Leaves, Black Widows Web of Poetry, Nimrod,* and *The Carolina Quarterly.* His earlier books of poems, *If Ariel Danced on the Moon,* and *The Strange Lives of Mr. Shakovo,* were published, respectively, in 2006 and 2008. He is married to pianist/voice teacher Nancy Townsend, with whom he is a gardening and hiking enthusiast.

ACKNOWLEDGEMENTS

Thanks to the following publications where poems first appeared:

The Buffalo News, "Rough Rockiness."
Nimrod, "Loomer."
Rooftop Poets, "Woman at Kitchen Window," "Ripple."
Elm Leaves, "The Common Man Encounters Divinity," "Near-Flight."